SO, YOU'RE A CHRISTIAN!
NOW WHAT?

SO, YOU'RE A CHRISTIAN!
NOW WHAT?

FINDING ANSWERS WHEN YOU DON'T EVEN KNOW THE QUESTIONS!

CATHERINE PAINTER

HENSLEY
PUBLISHING

6116 East 32nd Street
Tulsa, Oklahoma

HENSLEY
PUBLISHING

SO, YOU'RE A CHRISTIAN! NOW WHAT?
FINDING ANSWERS WHEN YOU DON'T EVEN KNOW THE QUESTIONS

ISBN 1–56322–104–7

ABOUT PHOTOCOPYING THIS BOOK

ACKNOWLEDGMENTS

Acknowledgments are always inadequate. I am indebted, however, to many individuals and groups who played crucial roles in shaping this labor of love:

Terri Kalfas, editor, and many others at Hensley Publishing whose interest and hard work brought this book to life;

My husband, Jack, my keenest supporter and constructive critic, who labored with me, whose sermons shaped my understanding of the gospel, and whose love sustained and energized me throughout the long process of writing this book;

Daughter Tamara, her husband Craig Peebles, their children Garrett and Caroline; and daughter Melanie, her husband Craig Hobson, their children Caleb, Catherine, Meredith, and Nathanael – cheerleaders all, who insisted I turn my dream into reality, and indulged my talking about the book three years without rolling their eyes;

My writers' critique group: Julie Boone, Katharine Parrish, Martha Van Der Linden, Dianne Waggoner, and Alice Wisler, who also encouraged and provided sounding boards for my ideas;

Cindy East, the first new Christian I mentored, whose urgent longing to grow spiritually inspired the outline and substance of the book, and whose hunger for God wouldn't let the matter rest;

The precious church congregations who graciously accepted me as their pastor's wife and provided me teaching and discipling opportunities that challenged my own spiritual development;

Tony W. Cartledge, editor, *Biblical Recorder*, Raleigh, NC, who provided my first, and additional, writing assignments;

Jerry W. Lemon, editor, LifeWay Christian Resources, Nashville, TN, who assigned me contracts for Sunday school curriculum;

The authors of Christian books and Bible commentaries that enriched my life and increased my knowledge of God;

I am deeply grateful to my parents, the late Leonard H. and Lola Peele Stephenson, for instilling in me the desire to pursue a godly life; and

Most importantly, I thank God for inspiring and entrusting me with this venture.

—Catherine S. Painter

To Jack,

Who excels in every way
in answering God's call to service,
who loves me,
believes in me,
and provides answers
whenever I know the questions

And to Tamara and Melanie,
who show me more about God
than I ever dreamed a mother could know

CONTENTS

Introduction..11

LESSON 1

Being Born, and Being Born Again..13
(Your New Life)

LESSON 2

Receiving a Name..29
(Christian)

LESSON 3

Learning to Trust...45
(Assurance of Your Salvation)

LESSON 4

Learning to Communicate..59
(With God in Prayer and Quiet Time)

LESSON 5

Learning to Feed Yourself..77
(With God's Word)

LESSON 6

Learning to Dress Yourself...89
(In the Armor of God)

LESSON 7

Bearing the Family Resemblance..105
(By Manifesting the Fruit of the Spirit)

LESSON 8

Assuming Your Role in the Family..121
(Using Your Talents and Spiritual Gifts)

LESSON 9

Learning the Family Rules..133
(What God Expects)

LESSON 10
Finding Your Hands and Feet..151
(*Serving Christ by Serving Others*)

LESSON 11
Learning to Share...165
(*Your Personal Testimony*)

LESSON 12
Learning to Walk..179
(*The Road that Leads to Life*)

LESSON 13
Learning to Talk...193
(*The Language of Christians*)

End Notes...201

INTRODUCTION

As I rummaged through an old trunk recently, I came across my birth announcement. Among other things, it stated my weight and length. For months my doctor probably observed me to determine whether my growth progressed normally. Concern to the contrary would have triggered immediate action; my parents would have considered no sacrifice too great. Had I shown no growth for nineteen years, I would have become the object of research; my story would have been written in medical journals and tabloids, accompanied by pictures of "the baby who never grew!"

In stark contrast, when I was born *spiritually,* I received little if any assistance to assure my growth as God requires *until we all ... become mature, attaining to the whole measure of the fullness of Christ* (Ephesians 4:13).

Perhaps because I accepted Christ as an adult, or because spiritual growth isn't visible to the natural eye, my condition went unnoticed. For years I wandered in a labyrinth of theological confusion. Years later I confessed this to a friend who asked, "Why didn't your minister husband provide answers?" My response was simple: "I didn't know the questions."

Then one day the Holy Spirit convicted me that God held *me* accountable for my growth. My husband Jack had preached from Luke 13:6–8 about the fig tree that failed to bear fruit, and I took it personally. Convinced that growth is what Christianity is about, I asked God for the additional year He allowed the fig tree to produce fruit. I had been a Christian too long to claim ignorance or blame others for my failure to bear fruit.

So, You're a Christian! Now What? is written for those who long for answers and those who teach believers who do. I have used *The New International Version,* but any modern translation is fine. It's important not to skip about in the book because the lessons are ordered with purpose.

Someone once said, "Growing old is mandatory; growing up is optional." God disagrees. He commands: *Like newborn babies, crave pure spiritual milk, so that by it you may grow up in your salvation, now that you have tasted that the Lord is good* (1 Peter 2:2–3).

Are you ready? Let's start growing!

BEING BORN, AND BEING BORN AGAIN

PHYSICAL BIRTH

You created my inmost being; you knit me together in my mother's womb…. Your eyes saw my unformed body.

— Psalm 139:13, 16

REFLECTING...

With seven children to provide for, my parents received the dreaded news: Mama was pregnant.

"Neither you nor the baby can survive," her doctor warned. "I know two places where you can go – one in the mountains, the other at the seashore. Which do you prefer?"

"I prefer to go home," Mama said. "God will see me through."

My birth was long and difficult. Born at home, I entered the world blue, with the umbilical cord wrapped around my neck … *but I lived, and so did Mama!*

"It's a miracle I saved her," the doctor said.

My parents knew a more powerful Hand had been at work, and gave thanks.

WRITE YOUR STORY

Write a paragraph titled "My Birth." If necessary, seek information from your parents or relatives concerning the circumstances and time of your birth. Name key people and places connected with your birth: parents, siblings, doctor, hospital, and the address of your first home. For interest, add some of your birth year's outstanding events.

_____

_____

_____

_____

SPIRITUAL BIRTH

Write John 3:3_____

_____

For years, I failed to understand the meaning of being "born again," that mystery that occurs the moment one receives salvation from sin and its consequences. Since Jesus compared spiritual birth to natural birth, it's good to consider what being *born again* does and does not include.

WHAT NEW BIRTH IS *NOT*

1. "Going Forward" During Worship

New Christians will certainly profess Christ publicly (Romans 10:9), but a profession of faith is only a "birth announcement," not the spiritual birth itself.

Jesus addressed the importance of publicly professing your faith. **Write Matthew 10:32–33.** Underline His promise once, and His warning twice.

_____

_____

While serving as counselor at two major evangelistic crusades, I was impressed by the number of people who "went forward" at the end of the service, but then left without Christ. They had been "seekers" only.

Matthew 19:16–22 describes a seeker who "went forward" publicly to the right Person and with the right question: "*Teacher, _____.*"

On what was this man depending in order to achieve eternal life?
___ Good works   ___ Moral upbringing   ___ Riches
___ Fine reputation   ___ Faith in Christ's atoning death on the Cross

Do you believe the man was born again during his encounter with Jesus?_____
What determined his decision to receive or reject Christ? _____
Check _one_ way his decision could be regarded as wise.
___He was free to live without boundaries or guidelines.
___He was young, with time to follow Christ later.
___He was not hypocritical.

Check _one_ way his decision was unwise.

___ He passed up being a famous disciple of Jesus.

___ His decision cost him eternal life.

___ His name was omitted from the gospel record.

2. Church Membership

Born–again individuals should join a church, of course. Having experienced salvation, we desire to _"grow up into him,"_ as Paul stated in Ephesians 4:15, since spiritual growth should follow spiritual birth as certainly as physical growth follows physical birth. Simply being in church, however, doesn't make people Christians. There is a difference between _professing_ Christ and _possessing_ Christ. Joining a church is a perfect first step for a new Christian, but church membership should be the _result_ of salvation, not an effort to achieve it.

Parents notify friends and relatives of their child's physical birth by sending out birth announcements. Christians announce spiritual birth by being baptized and uniting with a church.

Choose one. Describe your reason for announcing, or not announcing, your spiritual birth.

___ I have announced my spiritual birth by baptism and membership in _____ Church.

___ I haven't announced my spiritual birth, but I plan to do so on (Date) _____ at _____Church.

___ I've been born again, but I don't plan to announce my spiritual birth because

_____.

3. Assent to a Creed

Christians should choose churches whose teachings and governing practices are scriptural. However, giving intellectual assent to creeds and answering theological questions correctly isn't a guarantee that rebirth has taken place. Words like _grace, repentance,_ and _faith_ might be defined accurately, but head knowledge doesn't constitute regeneration.

As someone once said, "The distance between heaven and hell is eighteen inches – from head to heart."

Write James 2:19_____

4. Emotional Experience

When sharing my faith, I resist mentioning feelings that I experienced while accepting Christ. Describing my feelings could cause a person to reason that they should wait for that feeling in order to be saved. Emotions are valid, and do often accompany new birth, but God's Word, alone, is trustworthy.

The rich young man expressed dramatic emotion by running to Jesus when others weren't running, and falling on his knees when others weren't kneeling. Underline the emotion he showed even as he departed from Jesus.

Matthew 19:22 tells us, *when the young man heard this, he went away sad, because he had great wealth.*

List emotions and their results expressed in the following Scriptures.

SCRIPTURE	EMOTION	RESULT
Psalm 112:1–2	Praise and fear of God	He and his children are blessed.
Philippians 4:11–12	_____	(v. 13)_____
Proverbs 15:30	_____	_____
Proverbs 15:13	_____	_____
Luke 10:33	_____	(v. 34) _____

Can any of these emotions produce salvation? _____

Write Ephesians 2:4–5 _____

_____

> ❯ Who alone provides salvation? _____
> ❯ What great emotion has God expressed? _____
> ❯ What alone makes salvation possible? _____

5. Baptism

Christian baptism is an outward expression of the inner change that has already occurred in the born–again individual. In baptism, the spiritual newborn identifies with Christ and His Church. We are baptized, not in order to *be* saved, but because we *are* saved.

At the beginning of His ministry, Jesus approached John the Baptist for baptism.

Matthew 3:14 tells us John hesitated, saying:_____

_____

Jesus responded (in verse 15): _____

_____

Theologians have pondered Jesus' baptism, because John baptized for repentance of sin, and Jesus was sinless. Because the Jews believed and taught that descending from Abraham assured their salvation, Jesus grasped an opportunity to identify with the sinners He came to save. In the hour of people's new awareness of sin and search for God, Jesus, through baptism, became the model for all born–again believers. [1]

What did God say from heaven? (Matthew 3:17)

_____

_____

God's affirmation was a composite of two earlier statements. *[This is] my Son* was from Psalm 2:7, which all Jews accepted as a description of their coming Messiah. *With him I am well pleased* is from Isaiah 42:1, which defines the Messiah as a Suffering Servant. To Jews who were receptive to Jesus, the Lord's baptism presented two certainties: (1) He was their promised Messiah, and (2) the way before Him was suffering on the Cross. At Jesus' baptism, God set before Him both His task on earth and the way He would fulfill it. [2]

While the practice of baptism varies with denominations, baptism symbolizes the believer's identification with Christ's death, burial, and resurrection. Churches that baptize by immersion do so to fulfill the literal meaning of the Greek word *baptizo*, "total immersion in water," They interpret Romans 6:3–4 as a description of baptism by immersion. Candidates "buried" beneath the water exemplify death to their old way of life. Rising from the water, they *"live a new life."* Additionally, by exemplifying the death, burial, and resurrection of Jesus, they show through association with Christ that they, too, will rise.

Write Romans 6:4_____

_____

_____

Write Matthew 3:16_____

_____

_____

Keep in mind that regardless of mode – immersion, sprinkling, or pouring –water itself has no saving power. God's Spirit alone gives new life. If baptism could save, Jesus could have commanded it, and avoided the Cross.

WRITE YOUR STORY
MY BAPTISM

When:_____   Where:_____

Officiating minister:_____

Relatives and friends present: _____

_____

_____

Important details of the service:_____

_____

In **Matthew 28:19**, Jesus commanded that we be baptized:_____

_____

_____

Write Matthew 10:32–33

_____

_____

If you have professed Christ but haven't been baptized, why not schedule an appointment with your pastor to discuss an appropriate time when you can obey Christ's command?

6. A Good Life

As inspiring as good morals are, they don't qualify us for heaven. After Jesus stated God's commands, what was the man's response (Matthew 19:20)?

_____

_____

In verse 21, how did Jesus respond?_____

Regrettably, the young man went away without salvation.

During personal witnessing I'm sometimes told, "I'm as good as some members of your church." No doubt they're correct. Perhaps they're *better* than some church members; but goodness cannot save. We're wise to explain that while we are perfectly *saved*, we are not perfectly *matured*. Paul asked the Corinthian Christians, as he asks you and me, *"Don't you know that you yourselves are God's temple...?"* (1 Corinthians 3:16). Yes, we know; but our temples are still "under construction."

On this earth we will not achieve perfection, because we live spiritually in sin–prone bodies. We can be thankful that salvation depends not on our flawed goodness, but on the grace and mercy of a loving and forgiving God.

Complete Isaiah 64:6: *All our righteous acts* _____

_____

7. Good Works

If good works could save, Jesus could have drawn up a required list and bypassed the Cross. Even during Old Testament times, people weren't saved by keeping the Law. (See Hebrews 11.)

Complete Ephesians 2:8–9. *It is by*_____

_____

History records many well–intentioned efforts to earn salvation: Praying, fasting, penance, sacrifices, pilgrimages, church attendance, reciting Scripture, memorizing creeds, supporting charities, helping the needy – all powerless to redeem a person from sin.

Complete Titus 3:5–6. *God ... saved us, not because of* _____

_____

_____

THE IMPORTANCE OF GOOD WORKS

After saying in Ephesians 2:9 that we are saved, *"not by works, so that no one can boast,"* Paul continued in verse 10, "_____

_____."

So, we're saved not by works, but by God's grace through our faith that works. The way to salvation is by faith alone. Afterward, our lives produce good works, upon which our rewards in heaven will be based. (More about good works in Lesson 10.)

James 2:17 tells us_____.

List actions that give evidence that your personal faith is alive and producing good works.

Recent: _____

Ongoing:_____

Future plans: _____

8. Reform

We admire people who "turn over a new leaf" by sheer willpower, or by allowing the military, disciplinary schools and programs, or prisons to reform them. However, reformation cannot produce rebirth, for even if reformed persons never sinned again, reformation could not erase *past* sins.

9. Inheritance

Pastor Wayne Dehoney said, "In many religions, generation and faith are linked together. Babies born to Muslim parents are, by birth, Muslims; those born to Buddhist parents are Buddhists; persons born to Jewish parents are Jews. But persons with Christian parents are not born Christians. In order to be saved, the individual must be *born again.* [3]

Croft Pentz said, "Nature forms us; sin deforms us; school informs us; but only Christ can transform us."[4]

WHAT ABOUT YOU?

Was there a time before you invited Christ into your life when you depended upon something other than Jesus' death on the Cross to save you from sin? Explain.

_____

_____

WHAT IS THE NEW BIRTH?

Some find the term "born again" unfamiliar and perplexing, but Jesus Himself originated it.

A DIVINE MIRACLE

Being born again is reliving one of Creation's miracles. We who believe that Jesus is God's Son, and that His death on the Cross paid our penalty for sin, have spiritually reenacted

Creation's story. When we repented and placed our faith in Christ, God produced a divine change in our lives. We became spiritual creations the moment the Holy Spirit breathed into us, just as we became physical creations the moment God breathed His life into Adam on the sixth day of Creation.

Complete Genesis 2:7. *The LORD God* _____

_____

What does being *born again* mean? Perhaps a better question is: Does it really matter that we can't answer? Neither can we explain the creation of the universe, but we greet each morning, affirming the existence of another day. I can't explain the mystery of physical birth, but I live as a result of it, and I know it's real.

The moment we invited Christ into our hearts, His Holy Spirit entered and transformed our lives; and here we are.

Write 2 Corinthians 5:17–18.

_____

_____

When does new birth occur? The instant facts about God in our heads change to having His presence in our hearts. While we can't explain our receiving a divine nature and becoming new creations, we have been born again.

Read John 3:1–21. Nicodemus, a ruler of the Jews, sought Jesus and engaged Him in conversation. Jesus skipped the small talk and went straight to the point, saying in verse 3, *"I tell you the truth,* _____

_____

Verse 4. Nicodemus asked, _____

_____

Unregenerate people (those not reborn spiritually) often respond literally to spiritual matters.

Complete 1 Corinthians 2:14. *The man without the Spirit does not* _____

_____

_____

Write John 3:6–7. _____

_____

As if anticipating Nicodemus' next question, Jesus suggested that Nicodemus would know by experiencing the effects and results of his new birth.

Write verse 8. _____

_____

Jesus implied that new birth is a mystery we'll never fully understand, just as we can't understand the wind, but we accept the wind's reality by its effects.

William Barclay recalls a story by Dr. John Hutton about a workman who had been an alcoholic before his conversion to Christ. His fellow workers did their best to make him feel foolish.

"Surely, you don't believe that Jesus turned water into wine," one said. "I don't know whether Jesus turned water into wine in Palestine," he answered. "I only know that in my house He turned beer into furniture!"[5]

Barclay suggests that it's easy to discuss the intellectual truth of Christianity; but the essential thing is to experience its power. When a person undergoes an operation and is given medicine in order to be cured, he doesn't need to know the anatomy of the human body, or how the drug works. He accepts the cure without understanding how it was brought about.

At the heart of Christianity there is a mystery – not the mystery of intellectual appreciation, but the mystery of redemption.[6]

RESPOND

Read the Scriptures and describe their effects upon:

▶ **Your eternal destination, John 14:2: (Example)** *"In my Father's house are many rooms; if it were not so, I would have told you. I am going there to prepare a place for you."*
Effect: <u>My destination has changed from hell to heaven.</u>

▶ **Your secret thoughts, Philippians 4:8:** *Finally, brothers, whatever is true, whatever is noble, whatever is right, whatever is pure, whatever is lovely, whatever is admirable – if*

anything is excellent or praiseworthy – think about such things.
Effect:_____

▶ **Your behavior, 1 Peter 2:12:** *Live such good lives among the pagans that, though they accuse you of doing wrong, they may see your good deeds and glorify God on the day he visits us.*
Effect:_____

▶ **Your new nature's reaction to sin, Romans 6:12:** *Do not let sin reign in your mortal body so that you obey its evil desires.*
Effect:_____

▶ **Your new nature's ability to deal with sin, 1 John 1:9:** *If we confess our sins, he is faithful and just and will forgive us our sins and purify us from all unrighteousness.*
Effect:_____

YOUR ROLE IN SALVATION

Did you wait for salvation to happen to you? No. Scripture states clearly your role in being born again. While your physical birth occurred without your consent, spiritual birth depended completely upon your request to be born again. Interesting, isn't it? We cannot save ourselves, but we can condemn ourselves.

Why is this observation critical? Because without being *born* twice, we would have to *die* twice – physically and spiritually. The length of our physical lives on eternity's time line, if visible at all, would only be blips, while eternal life will continue, not just millions of years, but *forever.*

SPIRITUAL CHECK-UP

Review every step in your rebirth. Record the Scriptures, allowing God to review your salvation experience.

Check the steps you are certain you took in receiving Christ as your Savior.

1.   ___ I acknowledged I am a sinner.
Sin is going my own way. Acknowledgment of sin placed me under conviction, which awakened me to consciousness of sin, causing me to turn away from sin.

Romans 3:23: *for all*_____

1 John 1:8: *If we claim to be*_____

2. ____ **I confessed my sins to God.**

Confession is agreeing with God, saying, "Lord, You are right; I am wrong."

1 John 1:9: *If we confess our sins*_____

_____

3. ____ **I repented of my sins.**

Repentance is the 180-degree turn a person makes from going one's own way to going God's way. Repentance goes beyond conviction. Grieving over sin is conviction. Giving up sin is repentance. Repentance involves a change in direction and behavior. We all know people who are sorry for their sins, yet continue in them. They're convicted but not converted, because they haven't repented. Being awakened by an alarm clock convicts us that it is time to get up, but it's quite another thing to get out of bed! It's one thing to be convicted – awakened to consciousness of sin – but another thing altogether to do something about it.[7]

4. ____ **I now believe in Christ.**

Belief is accepting by faith that Jesus has forgiven our sins and that His spirit abides in our hearts. Which came first, belief or repentance? They may occur simultaneously.

John 3:16: *God so loved the world that*_____

Romans 10:9: *If you confess with your mouth*_____

_____

Since we are unable to believe something we don't understand, our minds must be informed.

Complete verse 17. *Faith comes from*_____

_____

5. ____ **My faith is now in Christ.**

Faith is taking God at His Word. It's an unqualified commitment based on evidence that goes beyond, though not contrary to, reason. Faith takes over when reason has run its course.

Bickel and Jantz say, "Some skeptics of Christianity are of the opinion that faith in Christ is only for those who are impressionable, ignorant, deluded, or naïve; and that 'faith' requires the willful suspension of intelligence. Nothing could be further from the truth. One is not saved by ignoring truth. Just the opposite. Faith requires belief (realization and appreciation) in the truth of the gospel – that Jesus is who He said He was; the Bible is true; and Christ is the way to salvation." [8]

Many skeptics agree that Jesus was the world's greatest teacher, healer, and miracle worker, but they don't believe in Him because they aren't trusting in Him for salvation.

Hebrews 11:1: *Faith is being*_____

_____

_____

If we could see that for which we hope, then faith wouldn't be necessary.

6. ___ I have received Jesus as my Savior.

Salvation is a free gift from God, but to possess it, we must receive it. Someone can offer us a gift; we may even *desire* it; but it cannot be ours unless we *accept* it.

Write John 1:12. *To all who received him,* _____

_____

_____

7. ___ I have assurance of my salvation.

Assurance is certainty with freedom from doubt. Salvation is deliverance from sin and its consequence.

1 John 5:13: *I write these things to you who believe*_____

_____

_____

NOW WHAT?

1. If you failed to check any of the above, settle them with God, and go your way rejoicing, assured that your salvation is secure, kept, and guarded by God.

2. Do you know someone who would benefit from the above exercise? Ask that person for permission to share the list with him or her this week.

Match the following definitions.

____	Salvation	1. Length and quality of the Christian's life
____	Conviction	2. Turning from going one's way to going God's way
____	Christianity	3. Agreeing with God: "Lord, you're right. Forgive me."
____	Eternal life	4. The unearned and undeserved favor of God
____	Confession	5. Acceptance by faith that Jesus has forgiven your sins and that the Holy Spirit dwells in your heart
____	Conversion	6. A personal relationship with Jesus Christ
____	Belief	7. Certainty with freedom from doubt
____	Faith	8. Awakening to a consciousness of one's sin
____	Repentance	9. Change in a born–again person
____	Assurance	10. Deliverance from sin and its consequence
____	Grace	11. Taking God at His word

Answers: 10,8,6,1,3,9,5,11,2,7,4

WHEN DOES NEW LIFE BEGIN?

For the prodigal son it was perhaps when *he ... got up and* _____. (Luke 15:20)

For Peter it could have been when Jesus asked, *"Who do you say I am?"* and Peter replied, *"You are* _____.*"* (Matthew 16:15–16)

For Thomas it was perhaps while touching Christ's wounds, exclaiming, "_____!" (John 20:28)

Many know the exact time and place they surrendered to Christ; others can't be specific. If you accepted Christ during childhood, your experience might resemble Timothy's.

Complete 2 Timothy 1:5. Paul said, *"I have been reminded of* _____

_____

_____.*"*

If you replaced the names *Lois* and *Eunice* with those of your parent and grandparent, would your story read like Timothy's? If so, you might not remember when you became a Christian. Having loved Jesus all your life, you recall only when you made public your decision to follow Christ. Your testimony won't be as dramatic as testimonies of people who received Christ after years of going their own way, but yours is a testimony all children would be blessed to share.

Complete Matthew 18:3–4: *He said, "I tell you the truth, unless_____*

_____

_____*."*

WHAT ABOUT YOU?

Your father and mother gave you physical birth. The Spirit of God and the Word of God gave you spiritual birth. First Peter 1:23 tells us Peter said: *"You have been born again, not of perishable seed,_____."*

Jesus emphasized in John 3:5, *"Flesh gives birth_____."*

Just as physical newborns don't instantly become adults, neither do spiritual newborns become Christ like overnight. Approximately 18 years are required for *physical* maturity; *spiritual* growth is also a process. While we have no PhD's from the "University of Spiritual Growth," we are on the way, growing *up into him who is the Head, that is, Christ.* (Eph. 4:15)[9]

RESPOND

Write a thank–you note to God for both your physical and spiritual births.

_____

_____

_____

Consider ending your prayer with David's petition in Psalm 139:23–24:

> *Search me, O God, and know my heart;*
> *test me and know my anxious thoughts.*
>
> *See if there is any offensive way in me,*
> *and lead me in the way everlasting.*
> *Amen.*

Signature _____   Date _____

RECEIVING A NAME

YOUR GIVEN NAME

A good name is more desirable than great riches; to be esteemed is better than silver or gold.

— Proverbs 22:1

REFLECTING...

Before ultrasounds revealed the sex of fetuses, many parents delayed naming babies until after they were born. Mama had chosen a beautiful name for me, but one made notorious by a famous seductress. Considering only the name's beauty, she disregarded, if she knew, the image it invoked.

Fortunately, my brother asked to name me. He loved our aunt's name. By chance, or God's intervention, I was named for her, and escaped a name that would have raised eyebrows, if not produced snickers, among our future congregations.

THE IMPORTANCE OF NAMES

The first question concerning a newborn is often, "Is it a boy or girl?" The next that invariably follows: "What is the baby's name?" Names connect us to people. Calling people by their names acknowledges them as individuals of worth, rather than anonymous faces in a crowd.

Names embody all that we are and represent. As a teenager, I rarely left home without my parents' caution: "Remember who you are." They didn't mean that I should remember my label of identification, rather that I was to uphold the name and reputation they passed on for me to safeguard. I sensed that should I dishonor the family name, I would answer not only to parents, but to God–fearing neighbors as well.

WRITE YOUR STORY

Write the story of *your* name. Your parents, siblings, and other relatives should remember details concerning the choice of your name, the person who named you, and for whom or what you were named. Include whether you like or dislike your name, and why.

If possible, define its origin and meaning. Is it historical, biblical, literary, ethnic, or an inherited family name? If you know the meaning of your name, does it accurately describe you?

I know a woman who named her sons for United States presidents. Is there anything unusual about *your* name?

Remember that while your surname was inherited, your personal name was a special gift that your parents hoped you would enjoy and treasure.

_____

_____

_____

GOD NAMED JESUS

You are to give him the name Jesus…

—Matthew 1:21

Just as our parents named us, so the Heavenly Father named His Son. In Matthew 1:18–25, we read that God sent an angel to Joseph in a dream to calm Joseph's fears concerning Mary's pregnancy.

Verse 20: The angel explained, "_____."
Verse 21: The name *Jesus* means, "_____."
Isaiah 7:14: What other name was Jesus given by God through the prophet Isaiah, and repeated in Matthew 1:23?_____

OTHERS GOD NAMED OR RENAMED

Genesis 5:1–3: Whom did God name?_____
Verse 2: Why was the name appropriate?_____

Luke 1:11–19: God sent the angel Gabriel to Zechariah to announce his wife Elizabeth's pregnancy, and to instruct Zechariah to name the baby_____.

Matthew 3:1: He was the forerunner of Jesus and later became known as_____.

Ancient Hebrews often devised names with significant meanings for their children, such as memorials to circumstances or past events. Pharaoh's daughter named the baby she discovered in the Nile River *Moses*, saying in Exodus 2:10, " _____."

God changed the names of some individuals to more clearly express His purpose for their lives:

Genesis 17:5: From Abram, meaning "exalted father," to _____ meaning "father of many nations."

Genesis 17:15: From *Sarai* to _____.

Genesis 32:28: From *Jacob*, meaning "one who supplants, or takes the place of another," to _____ meaning "a prince of God."

Matthew 16:15–18: To which apostle did Jesus ascribe a nickname from the Greek word *petros* (rock)? _____

Acts 2–4: Why was the nickname more appropriate for him in fulfilling God's purpose for his life? _____

Mark 2:14: Which tax collector for Rome answered Jesus' call to discipleship? _____

Matthew 9:9: After becoming a disciple, he was called _____

Read Acts 9:1–20. What persecutor of Christians heard the resurrected Jesus call his name on the Damascus Road? _____

Acts 13:9: After being converted to Christ he was known as _____.

GOD KNOWS OUR NAMES

Isaiah 43:1: Speaking through the prophet Isaiah, the Lord said, "*He who created you, _____*

_____

_____."

Exodus 33:17: God said to Moses, "*I will do the very thing you have asked, because_____*

_____."

Jeremiah 1:4–5: "*The word of the Lord came to me, saying, '_____*

_____

_____.'*"

Have you ever wondered why you were born? The Bible says that God created you and gave you life. Isaiah's words, *"he who formed you"* (Isaiah 43:1), assure us that God never abandons us. He molds us through experiences of joy and sorrow, prosperity and adversity. Even when we ignore His presence, He remains with us, quietly influencing us. God's reminder, *"I have redeemed you"* (Isaiah 43:1), is the most moving of His claims upon our lives. We belong to Him, not only because He created us, but also because He redeemed us. When we sinned, God, through Jesus' atoning death, redeemed us – bought us back – a point the Apostle Paul drove home in 1 Corinthians 6:19–20: *"You are not your own;_____

_____."* [1]

2 Chronicles 16:9 says *"the eyes of the LORD_____

_____."*

Because we are God's children, He hovers over us. In **Matthew 10:30**, Jesus expounded on the idea: *"Even the_____

_____."*

Perhaps during our youth, because we wanted independence and permission to go our own way, we felt smothered by our parents' watchfulness. Below, check feelings you have now concerning God's watchfulness:

___ I am comforted, knowing that God sees me at all times.

___ I feel threatened knowing that God knows everything I do and think.

___ I believe that God cannot take His eyes off me for reasons stated in Isaiah 43:4: I am precious and honored in His sight. He loves me.

Imagine! While God's watchfulness convicts us, the older we grow, the more precious His concern for us becomes.

God sometimes expressed His concern by calling people by name.

▶ **Read 1 Samuel 3:1–21.** Whom did God call repeatedly?_____

Verse 10: What was his answer? "_____."

Verses 19–21: Write three results of his listening to God.

    1. _____

    2. _____

    3. _____

▶ **Read Genesis 21,** the story of Abraham's son, Ishmael, borne to his wife's maidservant. Even though the idea had been Sarah's, after she bore Isaac in her old age, she regretted her earlier decision and became possessive of Isaac's inheritance. Fearing Isaac would have to share it with Ishmael, Abraham's son by her maidservant, Sarah sent Ishmael and his mother into the desert.

Genesis 21:14–20: God heard Ishmael's sobs when he and his mother feared they were dying. In **verse 17**, God called whose name? _____

Verse 18: What did God promise on Ishmael's behalf? *"I will_____*
_____*."*

▶ **Read Genesis 22:** Whose name did God call in **verses 1** and **11**?_____
How did he answer? *"_____"*

Verse 12: What did God command? *"Do not lay a hand on the boy…. Now I know that_____*
_____*."*

Verse 17–18: Because of Abraham's obedience, what did God promise? *"I will surely_____*
_____

… and through your offspring_____
_____*."*

▶ **Read Exodus 3:4.** Whose name did God call?_____
How did he answer? *"_____."*

Read Exodus 3–4. Moses was old when God called his name. Did he follow God's will as readily as the young Samuel did? _____
Which do you think is easiest – to hear and follow God during youth, middle–age, or old age?
_____ Why? _____

WRITE YOUR STORY

Have you had a "burning bush" experience – when you knew that God was present, revealing His will, saving you from harm or temptation, or healing you? Explain.

_____

_____

_____

_____

_____

_____

_____

During Israel's infancy as a race, God spoke audibly to people. As the nation matured, God spoke through the prophets. How do we hear His voice today? (See Hebrews 1:1–2.)_____.

GOD'S NAME

Our Redeemer from of old is your name.

—Isaiah 63:16

Read Exodus 3:13–15.

Verse 14: How did God identify Himself? _____ *God said to Moses, "This is what you are to say to the Israelites: '_____.'"*

There is more to the name *"I AM"* than meets the eye. By calling Himself *I Am*, God stated that He is and always will be the infinite and personal Lord who is behind everything, and to whom everything is ultimately traced. It's as if God said, "Oh, you want to know My name? I'm not sure why you need to ask, but if you insist, I am who I appear to be. There are no others like Me. My name is above reproach. When I promise something, consider it done." [2]

Verse 15: God also said to Moses, *"Say to the Israelites, '_____ _____– has sent me to you.'"*

Exodus 34:14: God called Himself one *"whose name is_____."*
Why do you think God described Himself that way? (See Exodus 20:4–6.)_____

_____

List names for God:
Isaiah 47:4:_____
Isaiah 63:16:_____
Amos 5:27: _____
Revelation 19:13: _____

THINGS WE ARE PRIVILEGED TO DO "IN HIS NAME"

Colossians 3:17: *Whatever you do, whether in word or deed, do it* _____

_____

Check and personalize things you frequently do in Jesus' name. Example:

_____ **Deuteronomy 10:8:** I _pronounce blessings_ in His name.

_____ **Micah 4:5:** I _____in His name.

_____ **Matthew 12:21:** I _____in His name.

_____ **Matthew 18:20:** I _____with others in His name.

_____ **Matthew 28:19 and Acts 19:5:** I _____in His name.

_____ **John 1:12:** I _____in His name.

_____ **John 14:13:** I _____in His name.

_____ **Acts 5:28:** I _____in His name.

_____ **Acts 8:12:** I _____in His name.

RESPOND

Recall something you did recently *"in the name of the Lord."*

_____

_____

_____

_____

End by personalizing Paul's words in Colossians 3:17: " _____

_____

_____."

Signature _____   Date _____

THE NAME ABOVE ALL NAMES – JESUS

Therefore God exalted him to the highest place and gave him the name that is above every name, that at the name of Jesus every knee should bow… and every tongue confess that Jesus Christ is Lord, to the glory of God the Father.

—Philippians 2:9–11

Paul said that everyone – believer, agnostic, atheist – will one day bow and acknowledge that *"Jesus Christ is Lord."* Rejoice! You have been born again; therefore, you will meet Jesus as Lord, not as judge.

Write what Matthew 25:34 tells you Jesus will say when He welcomes you into heaven:
"Come,_____
_____."

Read Matthew 25:41. With what three words will Jesus condemn those who refused to believe in Him? "_____."

While some believe that everyone will go to heaven, John disagrees. **Read 1 John 5:12:** *"He who*
_____."

GOD'S NAME, JESUS' NAME

"Before Abraham was born, I am!"

—Jesus, in John 8:58

You and I bear our earthly father's name. Jesus bore His Father's name. He said, *"I and the Father are one"* (John 10:30). When those who condemned Jesus asked, *"Are you the Christ, the Son of the Blessed One?"* (Mark 14:61), Jesus answered, *"I am"* (verse 62), identifying Himself by God's name from Exodus 3:14. Jesus claimed God's name many times.

Complete Jesus' "I AM" statements.
John 4:25–26: *"I_____am he…"*
John 6:35: *"I am_____."*
John 8:12: *"I am_____."*
John 10:7: *"I am_____."*
John 10:11: *"I am_____."*
John 11:25: *"I am_____."*
John 14:6: *"I am_____."*
John 15:1: *"I am_____."*
Revelation 1:8: *"I am_____."*
Revelation 1:17: *"I am_____."*
Revelation 1:18: *"I am_____."*
Revelation 22:16: *"I am_____."*

WHAT ABOUT YOU?

Read John 17:20–23. On the night before He died, Jesus had you and all who believe in His name, on His mind. In the Garden of Gethsemane, He prayed, *"My prayer is not for them* [His disciples] *alone."*

▶ For whom other than His disciples did He pray? *"…those who will_____*

_____."

▶ For what reason? *"… that all of them may_____*

_____."

▶ Why did Jesus want you *"in Him"*? *"… so that_____*

_____."

▶ Why has Christ given you the same glory God gave Him? *"… that they may be_____*

_____."

Knowing you were on Jesus' mind the night before His death, how do you respond?

_____

_____

WRITE YOUR STORY

Because Jesus prayed, *"May they also be in us,"* (verse 21), you, too, are privileged to use His name, *"I am."* Check statements that you personally claim as a Christian.

____ I am a believer in Jesus (John 3:16).

____ I am born again (John 3:3).

____ I am Christ's sheep (John 10:27).

____ I am the salt of the earth (Matthew 5:13)

____ I am the light of the world (Matthew 5:14).

____ I am a sinner (Romans 3:23) saved by grace through faith in Christ (Ephesians 2:8–9).

____ I am a fruit–bearer for Christ (John 15:8).

____ I am a witness for Christ (Acts 1:8).

____ I am a fellow worker with Christ (1 Corinthians 3:9).

Choose one of the above. Describe how you recently used one of your "I am" identities.

_____

_____

JESUS CALLS US BY NAME

In John 10:3–16 Jesus, described Himself as the Good Shepherd. In verse 11 He said, "_____
_____."

Proof that our names are important to God is found in Luke 10:20. Jesus promised, "*Rejoice that*
_____."

The Apostle Paul, in Philippians 4:3, referred to those who supported him in the gospel as "*my*
*fellow workers,*_____."

If you are a Christian, Jesus *calls you* "a Child of the King." It is God's desire for your name to
be associated with words such as *trustworthy, patient, forgiving, loving,* and *faithful.* [3]

RESPOND

Write a prayer entitled, "Lord, I'm Glad You Know My Name." Include benefits you have
experienced because of your personal relationship with Jesus. Reveal your nature to Him –
strengths and weaknesses. Confess any secret way you wrestle with His Word over some issue,
habit, or event in your life. Let God be the victor. (He is anyway!)

Agree with Him (confess) that He is right. Tell Him you're no longer running *from,* but *toward*
His love, knowing He is more concerned about where you're going in the future *in His name*
than where you drifted from Him in the past.

_____

_____

_____

_____

_____

Signature _____   Date _____

NICKNAMES

REFLECTING...

When I was tiny, my mother nicknamed me *Candy*. Upon entering school, my closest friends called me *Cat*. Not liking it, I wouldn't respond, and they dropped that nickname.

During college I became *Cathy,* a nickname I enjoyed for years. As we began our first pastorate, my husband Jack asked what I preferred to be called. I chose *Catherine* because it was the name I wanted to grow old with.

WRITE YOUR STORY

Have you ever been called by nicknames? Which did you like or dislike?

_____

_____

_____

_____

_____

Persecution can be exhibited through the use of derogatory nicknames. Jesus warned His followers that they would be *"persecuted because of* _____*"* (Matthew 5:10).

During my teaching career, I dreaded the annual Christmas party for faculty and staff. As the evening wore on, drinking increased, and jokes and laughter grew boisterous. On one occasion, after staying a respectable time, several of us thanked our hosts and left. The following morning a student rushed to find me.

"I overheard a teacher calling you a name. She said, 'We had a good time at the party last night after the Sticks in the Mud went home!' I knew she meant you."

Matthew 5:11–12 tells us Jesus encouraged His disciples, *"Blessed are you when people insult you …. Rejoice and be glad … for in the same way they*_____

_____*."*

WHAT ABOUT YOU?

What did Jesus call you (John 15:15)?_____

What did He nickname you (John 10:14)?_____

In your opinion, why? _____

Were you ever tagged with a derogatory nickname? Explain.

_____

_____

_____

_____

JESUS' NICKNAMES

Jesus was called derogatory nicknames such as *"winebibber"* and *"friend of tax collectors and 'sinners'"* (Matthew 11:19 KJV).

Read Mark 15:9, 12. During Jesus' trial, Pilate mockingly nicknamed Him "_____."
Read John 19:19–20. *"Pilate had a notice prepared and fastened to the cross. It read_____
_____ JEWS … written in Aramaic, Latin and Greek."*

The purpose for three languages may simply have been for people from all over the known world who were in Jerusalem for Passover to be able to read the charge against Jesus. However, since there were only three widely used languages in the world at that time, we may detect the providence of God in Pilate's madness.

Greek was the language of culture and science. Therefore, Pilate unknowingly proclaimed Jesus king over the realm of culture. Latin was the official language of civil law, government, politics, and was the language of the Roman Empire; thus Pilate proclaimed Jesus king over the realm of government and power. Hebrew was the national language of Palestine and the language of the law and the prophets. Providence declared Jesus king in the realm of morality, religion and the spirit. [4]

NAMES PEOPLE CALLED JESUS

Match Bible characters listed on the left to names and titles they called Jesus.

___ Nicodemus (John 3:2)

___ Martha and Mary (John 11:21,32)

___ Chief priests and Pharisees (Matthew 27:62)

___ The centurion (Mark 15:39)

___ John, the Gospel writer (John 1:1, 14)

___ Pilate (John 19:19)

___ An angel of the Lord to Joseph (Matthew 1:21)

___ The rich young man (Matthew 19:16)

___ Isaiah, quoted by Matthew (Matthew 1:23)

___ John the Baptist (John 1:29)

___ God (Mark 1:11)

___ Thomas (John 20:28)

___ The disciples in the storm (Luke 8:24)

___ Andrew (John 1:41)

___ The woman of Samaria (John 4:19)

___ Blind Bartimaeus ((Mark 10:47)

___ Simon Peter (Matthew 16:16)

___ Isaiah the prophet (Isaiah 9:6)

___ Haggai (Haggai 2:7)

___ Paul (Ephesians 2:20)

A. The Son of God

B. Rabbi

C. Jesus of Nazareth, King of the Jews

D. The Word

E. Jesus

F. That Deceiver

G. Lord

H. Master!

I. My Lord and My God!

J. My Son

K. Teacher

L. Desired of All Nations

M. Immanuel

N. The Lamb of God

O. The Christ, the Son of the living God

P. Wonderful Counselor, Mighty God

Q. Chief Cornerstone

R. The Messiah

S. Son of David

T. Prophet

Answers: B G F A D C E K M N J I H R T S O P L Q

RESPOND

Circle names and titles, in the above right column, that you are comfortable calling Jesus. Below, write a prayer. Address Him initially by the name you feel most comfortable with, and incorporate in the prayer other names you circled.

_____

_____

_____

Signature _____   Date _____

THE NAME YOU HAVE CHOSEN

The disciples were called Christians first at Antioch.
—Acts 11:26

The name *Christian* began as a derisive nickname. The word, which literally means "little Christ," was probably assigned to the disciples by outsiders in Antioch, Syria (now southern Turkey), due to public attention attracted by activity and achievements of the Church under its aggressive leadership there.

Antioch was the third–largest city in the world, surpassed only by Rome and Alexandria. Located fifteen miles from the Mediterranean Sea, Antioch was a cosmopolitan city noted for luxury, immorality, chariot racing, and the pursuit of pleasure with emphases on sports, gambling and nightclubs.

Antioch was famous for the worship of Daphne, the goddess whose temple stood five miles out of town, amid laurel groves. Legend held that Daphne was a mortal with whom the Greek god Apollo fell in love. To save her from his pursuit, Daphne was changed into a laurel bush. Priestesses of Daphne's temple were sacred prostitutes who led worshipers nightly in reenacting the pursuit, thus inspiring the phrase, "the morals of Daphne" to describe lustful living. It seems unbelievable that in a city of this kind, Christianity made great strides in becoming the religion of the world, proving there is never a hopeless situation.[5]

Evidently, Antioch pagans recognized that Jesus' disciples were so different that they labeled them *Christians* to distinguish Christ's followers from themselves. *Christian* is a common name for a believer today, but the title did not come into common use until the Second Century.

Certainly, no believers at that time would have been bold enough to assume a title embodying the name of their Lord. This is borne out by the fact that the name was never used by Christians in the book of *Acts*. Romans were probably responsible for the label, simply adding their "ian," meaning "belonging to the party of," to the Greek word "Christ." [6]

We can also assume that the nickname *Christian* was not bestowed by unbelieving Jews because *Christos* is Greek for the Hebrew title *Messiah*. Having crucified Jesus, Jews would not have used the title for their own Messiah to denote believers they regarded as heretics. [7]

In time, and by degrees, the name was adopted by the disciples and worn as an honor. By their lives they changed *Christian* into a name, not of contempt, but one at which all people would come to wonder. [8]

Paul reminded Christians in Ephesians 3:14–15: *"For this reason I kneel before the Father_____ _____."*

For this reason we bear our heavenly Father's name just as we bear our earthly father's name.

Acts 17:26. Paul said, *"From one man he [God]_____, that they should inhabit the whole earth,"* thus establishing our physical genealogy, dating from one man, Adam. In like manner, our spiritual genealogy dates from God through one man, Jesus Christ.

Acts 17:28. Paul continued, *"In him we_____ _____.'"*

Therefore, you and I are physical siblings with every human being dating back to Adam, and spiritual siblings with all who have believed in Christ, a line stretching from Peter, James, and John through the centuries to include the Christian you pass on the street, meet at the water cooler, and sit beside in church.

The name *Christian* appears in the Bible only three times. Write their meanings.

Acts 11:26._____

Acts 26:28._____

1 Peter 4:16._____

RESPOND

Meditate on what the name *Christian* means.

Consider the references you just read. Circle the meaning that most accurately defines you as a Christian today. Write a paragraph using the meaning you chose to describe the present stage of your Christian growth.

_____

_____

_____

Signature _____   Date _____

NAMES EARLY CHRISTIANS CALLED THEMSELVES

SCRIPTURE: TITLE:

Acts 6:3   "_____, *choose seven men from among you who are known to be full of the Spirit and wisdom.*"

Acts 9:32   "*As Peter traveled about the country, he went to visit the* _____ *in Lydda.*"

Acts 9:2   "*... so that if he found any there who belonged to* _____, *whether men or women, he might take them as prisoners....*"

1 Peter 1:1   "*... To_____, strangers in the world....*"

PONDER THIS...

Jesus' name separates Him from the millions of people the world has known. On a smaller scale, your name identifies and explains who you are. In neither your physical nor spiritual births did you name yourself: Your surname was inherited; your personal name was bestowed. But when you accepted Christ, you chose your spiritual identification.

Your spiritual name, *Christian*, not only defines you, it also helps define who you are to others. Today, as was true of the early Christians in Antioch, outsiders should see Christ in and through you.

Are there areas of your life that you want to improve in order to make your life a better testimony to the name of Christ? Write in light of Jesus' statement in John 15:8.

_____

_____

_____

NOW WHAT?

The journey toward spiritual maturity is a lifelong process. Your growth rate will vary from another Christian's in the same manner that one person's physical development varies from another's.

It's important to stay focused on Christ, remain steadfast in following Him, answer to the name *Christian* proudly, and, in all circumstances, *remember who you are!*

LEARNING TO TRUST

Trust in the LORD with all your heart and lean not on your own understanding; in all your ways acknowledge him, and he will make your paths straight.

— Proverbs 3:5–6

REFLECTING...

Throughout my childhood my father prayed before every meal, ending, "and save us in heaven for Jesus' sake. Amen." I wrongly assumed that we can't be sure of salvation until we're safe inside heaven's gate, and until then, some degree of doubt is normal.

Then, at nineteen, I invited Christ into my life to save me and live through me, speaking with my lips and ministering through me to others. I walked on air for weeks before doubt reared its head, smothered my joy, and drained my spiritual energy. I wondered, *"Suppose salvation doesn't 'take' with everyone?"* I was young, however, and busy getting my degree. I decided I would have to deal with my doubt later.

Later took years in coming. Once I questioned my husband concerning his assurance of salvation. Knowing that Jack became a Christian at nine, I assumed his profession of faith had been just a childish venture. He would surely understand my dilemma. Wrong!

"I have *never* doubted my salvation," he said, laying the matter to rest. "My favorite hymn is 'Blessed Assurance, Jesus Is Mine'. I want it sung at my funeral."

"What arrogance!" I thought. *"Isn't knowledge limited to past and present? How can he know the future?"*

He loved singing, "Heir of salvation; purchase of God, born of His spirit, washed in His blood."[1]

I sang along, my fingers crossed behind my back, secretly wallowing in the quagmire "where doubts arise and fears dismay." [2]

I was like a sick person unable to describe her symptoms to a doctor. I experienced a chronic, systemic feeling of unrest. As with other chronic illnesses, there were periods when my doubt went into remission, until some event triggered it, causing a painful relapse.

Clinging to my father's hope of salvation, I became a closet doubter, and, like a well–bred animal behaves when injured, I crept away to suffer alone. After all, who had ever known a pastor's wife who doubted her salvation? Flaunting doubt is fashionable today in some circles, but the demand in those days of ministers' spouses was nothing less than unwavering trust.

In secret, I plucked a spiritual daisy: "He saved me; He saved me not."

One night in frenzied wakefulness I screamed silently at Jack, "How can you sleep when I'm not even sure I'm saved?"

When he responded with quiet, rhythmic breathing, I hurled my anguish at God.

"Lord, if You're real, *do* something to assure me that I'm saved!"

God who "will neither slumber nor sleep" [3] answered, "I have. Did you not see the Cross?"

I visualized myself at a board game with Jesus. His pieces bore labels inviting trust; mine expressed doubt. Back and forth we played.

"Fulfilled prophecies" – "Whose?"

"Virgin birth" – "Really?"

"Parables" – "Explain."

"Miracles" – "Show me."

Jesus fingered His last piece, "The Cross." Gazing at me, He dropped it in place. The last move was mine. I gripped two identically shaped pieces; either would fit the remaining slot, ending the game. I stared at my choices: "Doubt" and "Trust."

Two images flashed through my mind – one recorded in Mark 14:61, when the high priest spitefully goaded Jesus at His trial before the Jewish Supreme Court, *"Are you the Christ, the Son of the Blessed One?"* and the Mark 8:29 account of Peter, who, when Jesus asked, *"Who do you say I am?"* answered, *"You are the Christ."* I studied both. One asked, "Are you?" The other exclaimed, *"You are!"* I would spend eternity in the company of one of them.

Trembling, I whispered, "My Lord and my God!" [4] and thrust my choice into place.

The game I would never play again was over...*and I had won!*

WRITE YOUR STORY

Check one:

_____   Since receiving Christ, I have neither doubted my salvation nor questioned Scripture. I trust God for all things, in all times and circumstances.

_____   Since professing faith in Christ, I have sometimes doubted my salvation and/or questioned some things God said or did.

If you checked the first, you are divinely prepared to strengthen others in doubt. Write, explaining your answer. Include appropriate scriptures if some come to mind.

_____

_____

_____

If you checked the second, confess your doubts and proceed with the lesson.

WHAT IS FAITH?

Hebrews 11:1 says, *"Now faith is_____*
_____."

Faith has no "maybe–so/hope–so" limits that I had placed on my convictions during my baby–Christian years. Faith places confidence in God's Word, regardless of circumstance or consequence. Not speaking from *self–confidence*, but *Christ*–confidence, Paul claimed, "I can do _____" (Philippians 4:13).

The night I whined, "Lord, do something to assure me of my salvation," I was admitting that I was indeed saved, but choosing to identify with the unbelievers who taunted Jesus: "*What miraculous sign then_____?"* (John 6:30).

Note the order of their request – demanding first to see in order to believe, requiring no faith at all. By fleshly standards, "seeing is believing," but with Christ, the reverse is true. Jesus insists, "Trust first; then you will see."

Paul wrote in Romans 10:17, "*faith comes from*_____
_____." My failure to know God's Word deprived me of joy in my salvation, and destroyed my motivation to share my faith.

WHAT IS DOUBT?

Doubt is uncertainty, *not* unbelief. One cannot doubt that which does not exist. While flinging my doubts at God, I was agreeing that His words and actions were real, and even confessing that I knew Him. Every doubter has at least glimpsed God, and many grow strong in faith. Alfred Tennyson said, "There lives more faith in honest doubt, believe me, than in half the creeds." [5]

FAMOUS DOUBTERS

Studying the Bible, I discovered there had been other devoted followers who had temporarily doubted God in some way.

Name the doubters:

Genesis 17:17	_____	"*Will a son be born to a man a hundred years old?*"
Numbers 11:21	_____	"*Here I am among six hundred thousand men on foot, and you say, 'I will give them meat to eat for a whole month!*'"
Judges 6:13	_____	"*If the Lord is with us, why has all this happened to us?*"
Luke 1:34	_____	"*How will this be … since I am a virgin?*"
Matthew 14:31	_____	"*Immediately Jesus reached out … and caught him….*" (sinking while attempting to walk on water)
John 3:4	_____	"*How can a man be born when he is old?*"
John 6:8–9	_____	"*Here is a boy with five small barley loaves and two small fish, but how far will they go among so many?*"
John 1:46	_____	"*Nazareth! Can anything good come from there?*" (upon learning that the Messiah was from Nazareth)
Mark 4:38	_____	"*Teacher, don't you care if we drown?*"
John 20:24–29	_____	"*Unless I see the nail marks in his hands … I will not believe it.*"

WHAT ABOUT YOU?

Describe a time when you expressed doubt. Perhaps you lamented with Gideon, *"Why has God allowed this?"* Or, like Peter, you were sinking physically, spiritually, morally, or financially when God reached out and saved you.

_____

_____

_____

FROM GOD'S WORD

Satan is a sore loser. Having lost our souls to Christ, he will settle for trying to steal our joy and witness from us by planting doubt in our minds. His first target was Eve, the crown of God's creation. Genesis 3:1 tells us, *"Now the serpent_____."*

It wasn't Eve's intention to doubt God. She was inspired by a source outside herself. Note Satan's craftiness in guiding her through a downward spiral into doubt.

1. Satan subtly planted a question in her mind (Genesis 3:1).
"Did God really say, 'You must not_____?'"
Satan resorted to one of his favorite tricks: misquoting God.
Write what God actually said in Genesis 2:16–17. *"You are free to eat from _____*

_____

_____.*"*

2. Eve doubted God's wisdom.
Satan's words, *"really say,"* insinuated that Eve heard God wrongly, thus planting confusion and doubt in her mind, placing her on the defensive. Notice how quickly she imitated Satan's style of exaggerating.

Compare **Genesis 3:3** with **2:16**. How did she exaggerate God's warning? *"You_____*

_____.*"*

Satan insinuated that God was selfish to withhold delicious fruit from Eve: God must want it all for Himself!

3. Eve doubted God's goodness and motive.

In Genesis 3:4, Satan said, *"You will not surely die.... For God knows_____*

_____."

4. Finally, Eve doubted God's honesty and agreed with Satan that God is a liar.

Write her action in Genesis 3:6._____

CAUSES OF DOUBT

▶ Limited vision

Paul provided a clue in 1 Corinthians 13:12: *"Now we see but _____*

_____

_____."

Corinth was famous for the manufacture of mirrors, but mirrors with today's perfect reflections didn't emerge until the Thirteenth Century. Paul's mirror was made of highly polished metal, and gave an imperfect reflection. [6]

We're told that infants do not see clearly immediately following birth. Neither do spiritual newborns. With our sight consumed by familiar things of earth, our spiritual near–sightedness delays our seeing and trusting God's long–range plan for our lives.

▶ Backsliding

Spiritual newborns easily slide back into the old way of life they know best. The older we are when we receive Christ, the more worldly ways we have accumulated that must be cast off. Just as physical babies never leap from crawling to walking without first learning to stand, neither do we take the leap spiritually.

Growth is a process that requires time. In 1 Corinthians 3:1–3, Paul spoke of the Corinthians' reluctance to grow in Christ: *"Brothers, I could not address you as spiritual but as_____*

_____

_____

_____."

While there is nothing wrong with being a newborn, there is much wrong in remaining immature. God expects us to grow, as Paul encouraged in Ephesians 4:13, *"until we all_____*

_____

_____."

Your interest in this book demonstrates your longing to trust God and reach the full stature of Christ.

▶ Failure to Understand Salvation

John Bisagno said that when a person becomes a Christian, the tendency toward sin, though forgiven, is not eradicated. That which has been forgiven has not been removed, else we would be perfect. Because of this, we continue to commit sins. It is correct to say that a Christian has *been* saved. But it is also correct to say that he is *being* saved. It is also correct to say that one day he will yet *be* saved." [7]

My father was right.

SALVATION'S THREE TENSES

PAST TENSE

From the moment we were born again, we were saved from the *penalty* of sin, released from fear and guilt, and justified (*"just–as–if–I'd"* never sinned). As the physical baby has no past but only a future, so does the spiritual newborn. When you were born again, your past sins were removed from your record and you were no longer accountable for them. They were transferred from your account to Christ's account when He died on the Cross.

Write Paul's assurances that your past sins are removed from your record.
2 Corinthians 5:17–19. *Therefore, if anyone is in Christ,* _____
_____
_____

Romans 8:1. *Therefore, there is now* _____
_____
_____

WRITE YOUR STORY

Paraphrase how God dealt with your past sins when He reconciled you to Christ. Personalize His promises by using pronouns *I*, *me*, and *my*.

Psalm 103:12 (Example): "*God has removed my transgressions from me as far as the east is from the west.*"

Isaiah 38:17:_____

Isaiah 44:22:_____

Hebrews 8:12:_____

Micah 7:19:_____

Isaiah 43:25:_____

PRESENT TENSE

Unfortunately, many Christians mistake the *beginning* of the Christian life for the *end*. They make a profession of faith; then sigh, "I'm glad that's over!" They fail to realize that it has only begun! A distortion of our evangelical tradition may be partly to blame for this. The importance of conversion cannot be overemphasized, but neither can the importance of Christian growth.[8]

We are *continually being* saved from the power of sin and set apart for a purpose. This is *sanctification*, a lifelong process. There are two natures at work within us. Paul wrote in Romans 7:15: *I do not understand*_____

_____

Remember, Paul confessed this after becoming a Christian! So, even saints can struggle with the old sin nature.

It's this struggle between our two natures that can keep spiritual growth on hold following our rebirth. I wrongly believed that born–again Christians didn't sin again; therefore, when I did sin, I feared I hadn't been saved after all. Doubt gnawed at my mind. I found no answer, because I didn't know the question, which was: "Now that I'm saved from sin (singular), how do I deal with sins (plural) that I continue to commit?"

WHAT IS SIN?

Sin is fleshly nature in opposition to God. *Sins* (plural) are the result of *sin* (singular). Paul insisted in Romans 3:23 that *all have*_____.
John echoed Paul in 1 John 1:8: *If we claim to be*_____

_____

Even on our best day, we sin – by commission, omission, or both. Sin was conquered at Calvary. We repented, and by the grace of God through our faith, we were born again. Daily, as we become more like Christ, our old natures surrender to His control; but they remain active within us and are cleansed only by daily confession of sins.

DEALING WITH SIN

First John 1:9 says, *if we*_____

_____

Confession is simply agreeing with God that He is right and we are wrong. We prevent sins from piling up by confessing them as they occur. This is God's plan for keeping us clean.

The person who "gets his ticket stamped for heaven," and willfully continues to go his own way is proving he was never saved. Judas is a perfect example of one who tasted salvation, but didn't digest it. Christians *fall* into sin; we don't schedule it. Once convicted by the Holy Spirit that we *have* sinned, we confess, repent, and forgive ourselves as God has forgiven us.

Once after I pled with a young man to give his life to Christ, he told me, "I agree with everything you say, and I want salvation some day, but I'm going to sleep with my girl tonight!" This was clearly not the voice of a redeemed person, but one whom the writer of Hebrews 2:3 warned: *How shall we escape if* _____?

In **Romans 6:1**, Paul asked, *What shall we say, then? Shall we go on sinning so that* _____ _____?

Living each day in step with Christ, we enjoy His fellowship through daily cleansing from sin through confession.

List three promises in 1 Corinthians 10:13 concerning sin.

_____

_____

_____

Our present is secure because we aren't holding on to Christ; He's holding us.

In **John 10:28–30,** Jesus promised, "*I give them* _____

_____

_____."

REFLECT

Do you continue to struggle against a fleshly desire to sin?_____

1 John 1:8: *"If we claim to be without sin,_____."*

Do you continue to experience life's difficulties?_____

John 16:33: *"In this world_____."*

Does Satan needle you about past failures and present unworthiness?_____

Even when he's right, we don't have to allow him to shake our confidence or rob our joy. We

have God's promise in **Hebrews 13:5:** *"Never will I_____."*

Which power is greater – the Holy Spirit within you, or the power of Satan? _____

1 John 4:4: *"You, dear children, are from God and … the one who is in you_____*

_____."

FUTURE TENSE

In heaven we will be saved from the *presence* of sin, the *glorification* for which my daddy prayed

daily for his family. One moment after death we will be with Jesus who promised in **John 5:24,**

"I tell you the truth, whoever _____

_____."

Our future is safe because we can never be condemned.

CAN YOU LOSE YOUR SALVATION?

God the Father says no.

John 3:16: *"God_____*

_____."

God the Son says no.

John 10:28: *"I give them_____*

_____."

God the Holy Spirit says no.

Romans 8:16: *"The Spirit himself_____*

_____."

Paul says no.

Romans 6:23: "The_____

_____."

John says no.

1 John 5:13: "I write_____

_____."

Peter says no.

1 Peter 1:3–5: "*Praise be to the God and Father of our Lord Jesus Christ! In his great mercy he*

_____

_____

_____."

Note the word *inheritance,* which means that our salvation, God's gift, is a settled and secure possession.

PONDER THIS

If eternal life could be lost, would it be *eternal*?_____

Linger with Peter's words in 1 Peter 1:3–5 that describe the security of your salvation.

First, it *"can never perish, soil or fade."* Second, it is *"kept,"* or reserved, for you in heaven. Third, you are *shielded* – a military term meaning "guarded and protected" by God's power.

REFLECTING...

As a new, immature Christian, my doubts were real, painful, and perplexing. I suffered mental and emotional guilt for doubting Christ who loved me enough to die for me. With God's help, I learned to trust Him by:

▶ **Deciding to have *faith*, rather than *doubt*.**

I rehearsed ways I *did* trust God, proving that He is who He says He is:

    I fell asleep, trusting I would wake.

    I trusted the sun to come up and the earth to remain in orbit.

    I trusted people's love; I could surely trust God's love.

❯ **Searching Scripture.** I noted famous doubters in Scripture. Since Jesus dealt tenderly with Martha and Mary's doubts at the death of Lazarus (John 11:17–44), and patiently encouraged Thomas, who doubted after being with Jesus three years (John 20:24–29), Jesus would surely be patient with me, His newborn Christian.

❯ **Acknowledging Satan as the source of doubt.** If Satan had been able to attack Eve by confusing her mind about God, he certainly considered me no challenge. Moreover, if Satan had attempted to conquer the very Son of God through temptations recorded in Matthew 4:1–11, he wouldn't hesitate to tackle me in his effort to weaken my faith and, thus, my husband's ministry.

I memorized Jesus' words in Matthew 4:10, *"Away from me, Satan! For it is written: Worship the Lord your God, and serve him only."* Afterward, when doubt reared its head, I spoke Jesus' command to Satan out loud.

NOW WHAT?

Do you trust God, regardless? Remember, Jesus holds you in the palm of His hand. You can never slip through His fingers.

Pearl Buck told the story of a monkey who became irked at God's protective care and decided to try the world for himself. Jumping as far as he could, he landed on top of a great mountain in a strange land, only to hear God's voice: "Little monkey, you have jumped only to the base of My thumb. You are still in My hand." [9]

On the day you were born, God placed you in the hands of a mother. When you were born *again*, God took you in His hand and placed you in the loving hand of Jesus. God has a double grip on you! Jesus said, *"My Father, who_____*
_____" (John 10:29).

While a group of botanists were exploring the remote regions of the Alps in search of new species of flowers, they discovered one they believed to be of such rarity that it would be valuable to science. Unfortunately, it was deep inside a ravine bordered by steep cliffs.

Then they noticed a curious boy nearby who was small enough to retrieve the flower. They offered to pay him if he would let them lower him into the ravine by a rope. The boy took a long look into the ravine and said, "I'll be back in a minute."

A short time later he returned, followed by a man. He said, "I'll go down and get that flower if this man holds the rope. He's my dad." [10]

RESPOND

Recall times when God "held your rope." He was trustworthy in the past; you can trust Him with the future. Complete the scriptures, personalizing pronouns with *I, me, my, You,* and *Your.* Father, I trust You always to be:

Above me, protecting.
EXAMPLE: Psalm 32:8. *I will counsel you and watch over you.*

Underneath me, supporting.
Deuteronomy 33:27. *The eternal God_____.*

Before me, leading.
Psalm 23:2. *You lead_____.*

Behind me, guarding.
Isaiah 52:12. *... you, the God of Israel,_____.*

Within me, teaching.
Ezekiel 36:27. *You have_____*
_____.

Around me, providing.
Matthew 6:31–33. *Do not worry, saying "What shall we eat?" or "What shall we drink?" or "What shall we wear?" For ..., your heavenly Father knows that you need them. But seek first_____*
_____.

RESPONSE

Pray through the above statements. Consider ending, "Father, You forgave my past, saving me from the *penalty* of sin; You protect my present, saving me from the power of sin; and You guard my future when, one day, I will be free from the *presence* of sin – *saved in heaven in Jesus' name!* Amen."

Signature _____   Date _____

LEARNING TO COMMUNICATE

I have sought your face with all my heart; be gracious to me according to your promise."
— Psalm 119:58

REFLECTING...

Some of my sweetest childhood memories are of quiet times with my mother when I nestled in her lap and fondled the soft skin under her chin. No words were necessary for communication. I simply eased into her presence and sought her face.

God longs for His children to communicate with Him. He woos us onto His spiritual lap, desiring that we seek His face. The chronicler said, *"If you seek him, he will be found by you"* (1 Chronicles 28:9).

For years I was the only person in our family without a scheduled quiet time with God. My husband Jack rarely began his pastoral duties without first seeking God's face. "I don't want to talk with people about Christ until I talk with Christ about people," he said.

Our older daughter Tamara confided, "When I end a day of teaching and start for home, I literally hunger and thirst for the Word of God." Spiritually outranked, I confessed that on my way home from school, I also hungered and thirsted – for popcorn and soft drink, a different kind of comfort food.

Melanie, our younger daughter, from early childhood resembled the deer in Psalm 42, who pants for water, and finding it, drinks, and is satisfied.

On one occasion I asked, "What have you learned new about God since we were together?" "How to wait for Him," she answered. "For years I read my Bible and prayed, and God never even showed up! Now I wait until He comes."

"How do you know when He arrives?"

"Mother! You know I'm here now, and before I came, you knew that I was not with you."

"Of course."

"It's simple. Meditate. Seek His face. You'll learn to distinguish between when He's with you and when He isn't."

I asked, "How do you maintain a daily quiet time?"

"I make an appointment with God the night before."

"Suppose I made an appointment but didn't show up?"

"Mother! You keep other appointments. Only a jerk would break an appointment with God!"

I had always believed in the power of prayer, often interceding for others and myself, but found it easier to believe in prayer than to *engage* in it. However, I promised God that I would meet Him the following morning at seven o'clock.

I arrived late and a bit nervous, looking as spiritual as possible with my Bible under my arm. I plopped down on the sofa. The longer I waited, the more foolish I felt.

Embarrassed and broken, I stammered, "Lord, I'm learning something about us: I don't know You. I've studied and taught the Bible for years, but You remain Someone I read about in a Book instead of a personal God who *'walks with me and talks with me and tells me I am His own.'*[1] I've substituted knowing *about* you for a personal relationship *with* You. Teach me to pray."

"Now I lay me down to sleep" came to mind, but didn't seem appropriate. Besides, it wasn't bedtime. Then I remembered the prayer Jesus taught His disciples. I prayed out loud, *"Father, hallowed be your name"* (Luke 11:2).

I felt the impact of 1 Corinthians 3:16: *"Don't you know that you … are God's temple and that God's Spirit lives in you?"*

I swallowed the lump in my throat.

How awesome – the God of the universe was with me. Not with some king or bishop – insignificant me! I simply called Him Father, and He came, just as my earthly father had come anytime I called. Waiting for God wasn't difficult. Melanie's voice echoed in my mind: *You'll know when He's with you, Mother.*

How had I expected God to prove His presence – by a heavenly drum roll?

WRITE YOUR STORY

Select a day when you were alone with a parent, guardian, or someone else who loved you very much. What made the time special?

_____
_____
_____
_____
_____
_____

God wants you to be alone with Him in the same way. Can you tell God, with the writer of Psalm 119:58, "*I have_____.*"

___Yes ___ No ___ I'm not sure what the verse means.

On a scale from 1 to 5, with 5 being most satisfactory, how do you rate your present prayer life?

    1   2   3   4   5

How often do you seek God's face?
___ I seek Him every day.
___ I seek His hand, asking for things, more often than I seek His face, praising Him.
___ I sought God once at a retreat when someone spoke on "Communing with God."
___ I seek Him occasionally, but I'd like to seek Him more often.

PONDER THIS...

While God has countless ways of breaking in on us, He places limitation on Himself by waiting for an invitation, having created us with free wills.

Jesus said in Revelation 3:20, *"Here I am! I stand_____*

_____I will come in ...."

How do you respond to Jesus' knocking?

    ___ I don't feel worthy of His presence.

    ___ I invite Him in on the basis of His Word, not my worthiness.

    ___ I've never given it a thought.

RESPOND

Pray on the basis of your above confession. Read Jesus' invitation in Mark 6:31: *"Come with me ... to a quiet place and get some rest."* Commit to one of the following responses:

___ I will continue my scheduled quiet time.

___ I will begin tomorrow

___ I'll think about it

Consider ending, "Father, I want to remain in the attitude of prayer, with my channel to You always open. Lord, forbid that You should knock and I not hear you. In Jesus' name, Amen.

Signature _____ Date _____

WHY QUIET TIME?

Paul wrote in Philippians 3:10, *"I want to_____Christ...."*

William Barclay said that while Paul had already discussed the surpassing value of the *knowledge* of Christ, in Philippians 3:10 he defined what knowing Christ means more specifically. The answer lies in Paul's use of the verb *to know.* As part of the Greek verb *ginoskein,* it indicates not intellectual knowledge of facts, theories, or principles, but the most intimate knowledge of another person. Clearly, it wasn't Paul's aim simply to *know about* Christ, but to intimately *know Christ.* [2]

Relationships grow through togetherness.

God loves hearing us pray.

The writer of Proverbs 15:8 said, "*The prayer of the*_____

_____." How often I rejoice when one

of my daughters or grandchildren approaches me to ask a favor, or simply to be in my presence.

God wants us to commune with Him as well.

Prayer is the shortest and only way into God's throne room.

The veil and space that separates us from God is penetrated as we pray. We enter silently into

His temple, and suddenly we are before His throne. There, too, we are in the presence of angels,

and with all the company of Heaven we worship and adore Him.[3]

Jesus, our great High Priest, takes our requests, approves them, and hands them to the Father.

Hebrews 7:25 assures us, "*He always lives* _____."

James 4:8 promises, "*Come near to God and* _____."

Since my first clumsy encounter with God, He has kept His promise.

WHAT IS QUIET TIME?

Be still, and know that I am God...

—Psalm 46:10

Quiet time is communing with God. Paul says in 1 Corinthians 1:9, "*God ... has called you into*

_____*our Lord....*"

What "good things" can become substitutes for quiet time?

___ Bible study

___ Attending religious seminars

___ Watching worship on television

___ Church work

___ Volunteering for worthy causes

___ Other _____

WHY SEEK GOD'S FACE?

Alexander MacLaren said, "God knows our needs before we ask. Then what is prayer for? Not to inform Him, nor to move Him, unwilling, to have mercy, as if like some proud prince He requires recognition of His greatness as the price of His favors. Prayer fits our hearts' need to receive gifts, which He is ever willing to give, but which we are not always fit to receive. As Saint Augustine phrased it: 'The empty vessel is by prayer carried to the full fountain.'" [4]

TALK TO GOD ABOUT IT

God says in Psalm 4:4: *"Search your hearts and be silent."*

When we experience dry spells and God seems silent or unapproachable, we need only to search our hearts for the reason. Someone asked, "When you and God seem far apart, who moved?" Hebrews 13:8 assures us that *Jesus Christ is*_____
_____. Isaiah 59:2 expands the idea: *Your iniquities* _____.

Answer and underline the provisional phrases that often begin with *if*.

1. Are all your known sins confessed? ___ Yes ___ No ___ Not sure
Solution: 1 John 1:9. *If we confess our sins, he is faithful and just and will forgive us our sins and purify us from all unrighteousness.*
Procedure: Paul said in Colossians 2:11–14 that your past sins were cancelled when you accepted Christ. In that moment, God justified you – by forgiving your sins and removing them from your record, as though they had never happened (just–as–if–I'd never sinned). **That is salvation.**

Yet sometimes we have difficulty forgiving ourselves. Or, perhaps we neglect to confess times when we sin after becoming a Christian. Both of these can hamper our Christian walk.

We should never carry the burden of a forgiven sin; neither should we ignore sin when it occurs after we accept Christ. We must learn to accept God's forgiveness for past sins. But we must also learn to confess our sins daily, seek God's forgiveness, and go forward, knowing He has forgiven us.

How can we do this? Go aside with pen and paper. Write each sin the Holy Spirit brings to your mind that you have committed and not confessed since becoming a Christian.

Confession requires naming the sin. Satan will encourage you to justify yourself. Resist him. Agree with the Holy Spirit as He convicts you. Confess, "You're right, Lord."

Now, add each sin you have difficulty forgiving yourself for that occurred before you accepted Christ.

<u>Do not share your list with anyone.</u> Write across the page, "Jesus paid it all," or "1 John 1:9." Destroy the paper. Tear it up or burn it, and forgive yourself.

Why not share your list? Because God is the Person you sinned against. In Psalm 51:4, David said, "*Against_____in your sight....*"

For me this exercise was the most fruitful hour of my Christian experience. Later, as the Spirit reminded me of sins I had overlooked, I confessed them; and, putting them behind me, I forgave myself.

Then I could pray with the psalmist in Psalm 19:12–13: *Forgive my hidden faults.*_____
_____. Amen

2.   Are you seeking God's agenda and not your own? ___ Yes ___ No ___ Not sure
Solution (if your answer is no): 1 John 5:14: *"This is the confidence we have in approaching God: that if we ask anything according to his will, he hears us."* Our prayer must be one that Jesus can sponsor and endorse.

3.   Are you trusting God, despite outward circumstances? ___ Yes ___ No
Solution (if your answer is no): Romans 8:28: *We know that in all things God works for the good of those who love him, who have been called according to his purpose.*

4.   Are you right with others? ___ Yes ___ No
Check relationships that are not quite right:
___ God ___ Spouse ___ Parents ___ In–laws ___ Siblings ___ Pastor ___ Neighbors
___ Employer ___ Employee ___ Competitors ___Enemies

Solution: On your list, which sins are against God alone? Confess them and make it right with Him. Where sins are against another, confess them to God and make things right with that person. Where sins are against a group, confess them to God and make things right with the group.

Are you obsessed by sins others have committed against you? Claim Colossians 3:13: *Bear with each other and*_____

_____.

Did you remember to underline the provisional phrases in numbers 1–3?
Review the responses you checked in number 4.
Write Scriptures that offer help._____

_____

With your heart prepared, write and claim God's two–fold promise in Proverbs 8:17:

_____

A SUITABLE TIME

When did the following people meet with God?

Abraham (Genesis 19:27)   _____ *Abraham got up and returned to the place where he had stood before the* LORD.

David (Psalm 5:3)   _____, *O* LORD, *you hear my voice* ....

Moses (Psalm 90:14)   *Satisfy us* _____ *with your unfailing love*....

Ezekiel (Ezekiel 12:8)   _____ *the word of the* LORD *came to me.*

Jesus (Mark 1:35)   _____ *Jesus got up ... and went off to a solitary place, where he prayed.*

What benefits result from seeking God in the morning?
___ I receive instructions for my day.
___ I give Him the best part of my day.
___ I don't go through the day without His help.
___ I am more alert after resting.

Some Christians seek God at times other than morning. Today's pressures and circumstances differ from those in Bible times. God is eager to meet us *whenever* we approach Him.

If you meet with God in the evening, regard your quiet time as a spiritual head start on the next day. Motive is the key. Underline the psalmist's motive when he wrote, *I seek you with all my heart; do not let me stray from your commands* (Psalm 119:10).

What do you hope most to gain from quiet time?

_____

_____

A SOLITARY PLACE

Mark 1:35 records that Jesus _went off to_____, _where he prayed._
Jesus instructed in Matthew 6:6, "_When you pray, _____
_____ to your Father...._"

Jesus prayed alone. Mark 6:46 tells us, _After_____
_____.

Again, in Matthew 14:23, we read, _After he had dismissed them, he_____
_____.

Finding the perfect place for privacy might not happen. One young man often has quiet time in his office while others go to lunch. Another prays in his car before leaving for work. Quietness is necessary for God to preserve our spiritual health. On our busiest day we can find a solitary place where God can "smooth out the wrinkles of our souls." Jesus promises to meet us there. He said in Matthew 11:28, "_Come to me,_____
_____."

REFLECTING...

My keeping a regular quiet time resulted from an act of my will, not my emotions. Frankly, when I first began to do this, I didn't "feel" like praying early in the morning; yet I knew that if I waited until I felt like praying I would never pray. Jesus revealed the reason in Matthew 26:41: "_The spirit is willing, but_____._"

I placed my clock where I had to get out of bed to turn off the alarm. Then I took my shower and dressed in order to feel awake. Because I rose earlier than my husband, I had the breakfast room to myself. Achieving fifteen minutes with God required scheduling additional time because Satan distracted me, pointing out things I should be doing. There were valid distractions, too.

Soon, my quiet time became the starting point for my day, when I drew from God's sufficiency to fill my emptiness. I lengthened my prayer time when the Spirit impressed upon me to pray for my students by name. With five classes, I prayed for one class each weekday, leaving other causes for weekends.

My quiet time affected my classroom environment. When students became uncooperative, or confrontational, I chose private moments to share my prayer habit with them including the day of the week I prayed for them by name. As word spread that I prayed for them, their love and respect for me increased, as did mine for them, and the atmosphere grew sweet.

WRITE YOUR STORY

Choose one.
Describe a time when prayer changed you, resulting in change in others.

_____

_____

_____

_____

_____

_____

Describe a present situation in which you will allow prayer to work for change.

_____

_____

_____

_____

_____

_____

Prayer can become such a priority in our lives so that we begin to pray *"continually"* (1 Thessalonians 5:17). This doesn't mean staying on our knees all day. It means living in an attitude that keeps communication with God open. The Spirit longs for our companionship. *Because* _____ (Psalm 116:2).

DEVELOP A PLAN

Without a plan, quiet time can become a begging session. The following visual includes ten elements of worship, designed by Waylon B. Moore, Missions Unlimited, Inc., Tampa, Florida. Dr. Moore was among the first to stress discipleship for maturing Christians.

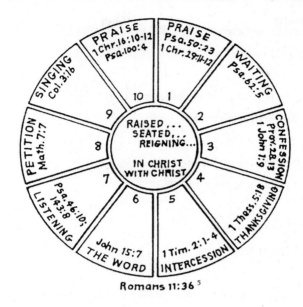

Romans 11:36 [5]

With segments divided equally into six minutes, the plan requires an hour. When divided into three–minute segments, it uses thirty minutes. Divide the time to fit your schedule. When I'm limited to fifteen minutes, I choose portions I feel the greatest desire or need for, or reduce the time spent in each.

1. PRAISE

*"I will*_____*"* (Psalm 9:1).

Praise honors God's person, nature, and attributes. The psalmist advised, *"Enter ... his courts* _____*"* (Psalm 100:4).

The morning I prayed, *"hallowed be your name,"* I was praising God. Because God answers prayer that honors His name, I never omit praise. Should time run out, I have done the most important thing. God wants us to thank Him for all He does, and praise Him for who He is. Can you praise Him even when things go wrong? ___ Yes ___ No ___ Not sure

Read Psalm 13. Circle the verses that describe the way you perceive your life at the present time.

> [1] *How long, O LORD? Will you forget me forever?*
> *How long will you hide your face from me?*
>
> [2] *How long must I wrestle with my thoughts*
> *and every day have sorrow in my heart?*
> *How long will my enemy triumph over me?*

³ Look on me and answer, O LORD my God.
Give light to my eyes, or I will sleep in death;

⁴ my enemy will say, "I have overcome him,"
and my foes will rejoice when I fall.

⁵ But I trust in your unfailing love;
my heart rejoices in your salvation.

⁶ I will sing to the LORD,
for he has been good to me.

In which verses did the psalmist praise God regardless of circumstances?_____

2. WAITING

Be still before the LORD and wait patiently for him....

—Psalm 37:7

Picture Jesus and look into His face by faith.

3. CONFESSION

I acknowledged my sin to you and did not cover up my iniquity.

—Psalm 32:5

Proverbs 28:13: *He who conceals his sins does not prosper, but* _____
_____

Remember, as we learned earlier, the Holy Spirit indwells every Christian, convicting us when we sin. Allow Him to remind you of thoughtless words, attitudes, and reactions that you have not confessed. Be honest. Don't bluff. Claim His forgiveness and thank Him for it by faith, not feelings. Then remember to forgive yourself. ⁶

When you confess a sin as it occurs, claiming 1 John 1:9, you continually live a cleansed life. Spiritual "garbage" cannot collect.

4. THANKSGIVING

*Enter his gates*_____

_____. Psalm 10:4.

Thank God for what He is doing in you, with you, and around you. Thank Him for things you often take for granted. Reflect on the past and thank Him for results, victories, and answered prayers.[7]

5. INTERCESSION

Intercession is prayer on behalf of: friends, family, church, neighbors, missionaries, world leaders and events. Name them along with specific concerns for them.

6. THE WORD

Go deeply into a short passage rather than skim a large portion when you are without sufficient time to delve into its meaning. Bible *study* is invaluable to spiritual growth, but your quiet time is not the proper time for it.

Choose a psalm, a parable, a prayer, or other short passage. Link the scripture to your life. Pray the passage back to God, telling Him how you will respond.

7. LISTENING

Listening is letting God's Word echo in your heart. Ask, "What is your message for me, Lord? Is there a promise here? A warning? A command? An example to follow or refute? Information You want me to know?"

Give the Spirit time to reveal what God is saying to you through His Word.

8. PETITION

Petition is praying for your own needs, such as

Give us today our _____(Matthew 6:11).

or direction:

Show me _____(Psalm 143:8).

Remember:

>You are coming to a King; great petitions with you bring.
>
>For His grace and power are such, none can ever ask too much. [8]

9. SINGING

Psalm 96.

My mother–in–law died during her quiet time with God. Her daughter heard her singing, *"Oh, how I love Jesus, O how I love Jesus, O how I...."* When the singing stopped abruptly; she rushed to discover that her mother had gone to be with the One she loved.

The psalmist said, in Psalm 100:2, *"Worship the LORD with gladness; _____ _____."*

One of my most valued tools during quiet time is my hymnbook. Using the topical index, I find songs to fit every need and desire of my heart. I often fall asleep at night praising God in song. The psalmist insisted in Psalm 98:1, *"Sing to the Lord_____ _____...."*

10.   PRAISE

Beginning and ending quiet time with praise is intentional. Review God's works, wonders, and miracles. Praise Him again for who He is, and thank Him again for all He does.

DANIEL'S MODEL PRAYER

Read Daniel 9:4–19. Which verses do you believe contain:

1. Praise:_____

2. Confession: _____

3. Intercession:_____

4. Petition: _____

5. The Word (verses revealing Daniel's knowledge of God's Word):_____

6. Which elements of the Visual on page 69 does Daniel's prayer not include, but imply?

_____

_____

_____

WHEN GOD DOESN'T SEEM TO ANSWER

As a baby Christian, I wanted a clear "yes" or "no" from God, or I would assume that He hadn't answered my prayer. Now I know that God always answers. Psalm 34:15 tells us, *The eyes of the Lord are_____cry;....*
The truth was that I didn't like His answer, and therefore I failed to recognize it when it came.

God's answers can be:

Direct

God says yes or no immediately, leaving no question in our minds.

Delayed

God sees the beginning and ending of all things, and answers in His own time and way. He doesn't operate on earth's timetable; in fact, God doesn't exist in time. *With the Lord a day is like* _____(2 Peter 3:8).

Sometimes God must first work things out in others' lives and circumstances before answering our prayers.

Evelyn Christenson believes that God deliberately delays answering some prayers so that there will be no doubt concerning who receives credit for what happens. After we have exhausted all human resources, then God answers, so that we recognize that the answer came from Him.[9]

Different

As a teenager I prayed that I would marry a rich man. God did give me a rich husband, but one who is rich in things eternal, not in things of the world. Perhaps you, too, are grateful for some prayer that God answered differently from what you expected.

> An unknown soldier expressed it well:
> I asked God for strength that I might achieve,
> But I was made weak that I might learn humbly to obey.
> I asked for health that I might do greater things.
> I was given infirmity that I might do better things.
> I asked for riches that I might be happy.
> I was given poverty that I might be wise.
> I asked for power that I might have the praise of men.
> I was given weakness that I might feel my need of God....

I got nothing that I asked for

But everything I hope for.

Almost despite myself my prayers were answered.

I am among all men most richly blessed. [10]

With which lines do you identify most?

_____

_____

Denied

Isaiah 59:2 says, "*Your iniquities have*_____."

The psalmist agreed: "*If I had cherished sin in my heart,*_____

_____" (Psalm 66:18).

This doesn't mean that we must be sinless before God hears us. If we waited to become morally perfect, no one would pray. The sinner that God refuses to hear is the person who enjoys sin, repeats it, and refuses to confess and turn away from it. This person short–circuits his own request, because God's holiness will not and cannot coexist with sin.

Solution: Memorize and exercise 1 John 1:9.

WRITE YOUR STORY

How has God answered a specific prayer *recently* in your life?

Direct: _____

Delayed: _____

Different: _____

Check needs for God's comfort that you are presently experiencing:

____ Rejection ____ Important decision ____ Lost income ____ Undue stress

____ Serious illness ____ Passed over for promotion ____ Other _____

Solution: Psalm 34:18: *The LORD is*_____.

Praise God anyway, agreeing with Habakkuk 3:17–19:

> *Though the fig tree does not bud and there are no grapes on the vines, though the olive crop fails and the fields produce no food, though there are no sheep in the pen*

and no cattle in the stalls, yet I will rejoice in the LORD, I will be joyful in God my Savior. The Sovereign LORD is my strength, he makes my feet like the feet of a deer, he enables me to go on the heights.

Praying in this manner, you will reach the heights and agree with Job: *Though_____*

_____(Job 13:15).

NOW WHAT?

Determine by your will, not your feelings, to seek God's face daily.

Isaiah 55:6: *Seek_____.*

Don't allow your soul to grow tired and your spiritual power to grow faint. Accept Christ's invitation in Mark 6:31: *Come with me ... to a quiet place and get some rest.* And don't wait for a heavenly drum roll!

LEARNING TO FEED YOURSELF

Like newborn babies, crave pure spiritual milk,
so that by it you may grow up in your salvation
now that you have tasted that the Lord is good.
— 1 Peter 2:2–3

REFLECTING...

Early in our dating relationship, Jack took me to his church's youth fellowship. He had been attending church since infancy. I was a new Christian, still uncomfortable in Christian groups. But we were seniors in college, and Jack wanted his friends to know me before we graduated.

As Jack introduced me, they perhaps assumed I was as spiritually mature as he; otherwise, why would a future minister be interested in me? They would soon discover the truth when someone suggested a Bible quiz.

Why had I not suspected that Christians might play something silly like a Bible game? I should have insisted on a movie!

We divided into two competing rows. The row with the player who remained longest won. I was seated first in one of the rows.

"How many testaments are in the Bible?" the leader asked.

Luck was with me – two, of course – the Old and New!

"Two!" someone shouted from the opposite row.

My cheeks burned. I was *Jack's girl,* and he was president of this outfit!

"How many books are in the Bible?"

I watched as their heads leaned forward like dominoes, encouraging me. Funeral-parlor silence ensued while eternity passed. Stumped by the most elementary question, I pushed my chair out of line and listened while their voices peppered the air with questions and answers progressing from simple to difficult, all sounding like Greek to me.

Sitting there, I recalled receiving a Bible for Christmas when I was ten and struggling through *Genesis* and *Exodus* before getting "buried in the graveyard of *Leviticus*." The Old Testament appeared to be about nomads with names I couldn't pronounce, wandering around in a country I couldn't find on the map!

After serving two years in the Air Force, Jack "robbed the spiritual cradle" and married me. He entered seminary and I taught music to support us. I was on the fast track to becoming a minister's wife with virtually no Bible knowledge. No doubt Jack would have supplied answers had I known the questions, but he seemed totally unaware of the extent of my scriptural illiteracy. Was I a good actress!

Had I been *physically* starving in some third world country, people's hearts and purses would have opened to me, but as the spiritually malnourished person I was, I was overlooked.

Jack Kuhatschek says that we view someone who is mentally retarded as "abnormal." Yet we accept spiritual retardation as normal. He claims that our churches are full of Christians who have known the Lord for many years, who have not grown spiritually as they have aged chronologically. They are spiritual infants in physical adult bodies.[1]

I was one whom the writer of Hebrews 5:11–14 described well:
You are slow to learn. In fact, though by this time you ought to be teachers, you need someone to teach you the elementary truths of God's word all over again. You need milk, not solid food! Anyone who lives on milk, being still an infant, is not acquainted with the teaching about righteousness. But solid food is for_____

_____.

That was my situation: I was subsisting on milk. Determined that Hebrews 5:11–14 would never again reflect my spiritual condition, I purchased a small spiral-bound calendar, each page containing one verse of scripture, and, infant-like, I nibbled on spiritual crumbs that year.

Undernourished, I progressed to devotional books. With short messages including Scriptures endorsing the writers' thoughts, I snacked on passages that skipped randomly through the Bible. I had never read any other book so haphazardly.

Jack was filling his library with commentaries and books by famous preachers and leading theologians. Like a starved animal, I devoured them. At least I had progressed from nibbles and snacks to full–course meals. However, reading books about the Bible left me feeling no need to read the Bible itself.

Years later, as I sat reading on a beach, the Spirit whispered, "When will you read My Book?" I visualized myself in heaven's courtroom before a disappointed God whose book I had read only in bits and snatches, and even then, through others' interpretations.

Under conviction, I promised God I would read from Genesis to Revelation under the Spirit's guidance alone, enabled to say with the psalmist, "I have not departed from your laws, for___

_____." [2]

Within a year I completed my first reading and started over with commentaries and Bible dictionaries to enlarge my understanding. Before long I felt undernourished when I skipped even one day. It was the most exciting year of my spiritual life!

WHAT ABOUT YOU?

Assess your method of reading the Bible.

_____ I don't read it.

_____ I don't feel qualified to interpret what I read; I let professionals spoon–feed me.

_____ I "nibble" on my pastor's sermon texts.

_____ I "snack" on scriptures in devotional books.

_____ I follow a definite "meal plan" without questioning or tampering with texts, or depending on others for interpretation.

If you checked the final choice, describe your plan.

_____

_____

RESPOND

Praise God for His Word. Thank Him that you live where you are free to read and obey it.

Personalize Job 23:12: "*I have not* _____

_____."

Signature _____   Date _____

If you checked one of the first four choices as your method of reading the Bible, don't despair. Determine why you're not feeding yourself spiritually. There must be a reason. Try to find it below.

True/False:

____ I can't find time. God understands that I'm occupied with other matters.

____ God's book is too long.

____ I might not live up to God's commands. I wouldn't want to disappoint Him.

____ I already know right from wrong.

Note: All answers should be false. If you answered "True" to any, God disagrees.

Write and claim His solution in Philippians 4:13 for your reluctance, if any, to practicing consistent Bible reading: _____

WHAT IS THE BIBLE?

Check <u>one</u> appropriate answer. The Bible is:

____ a story with beginning and ending, revealing God's redemptive plan for our lives

____ a book easily read in seventy hours.

____ a compilation of law, history, philosophy, ethics and prophecy, written by individuals in a variety of themes and styles across centuries, yet expressing unity.

____ God's operational manual for life, providing nutrition for continuous spiritual growth

____ all of the above   **Last answer is correct.**

NOW WHAT?

1. Commit to a regular plan. Consider a prayer similar to the one I prayed while under conviction to read God's Word: Father, I acknowledge my sin of not reading The Bible. You said in Deuteronomy 8:3, "…*man does not live on bread alone but*_____ _____." I confess that I've been getting by on the power of flesh rather than drawing strength from Your Word. On the basis of 1 John 1:9, I accept Your forgiveness, and denounce every sinful excuse that keeps me from Your book: lack of interest, laziness, pleasure in secondary things, sleepiness, and anything preventing my knowing Your will for my life. In Jesus' name, Amen.

Signature _____   Date _____

2. **Stay with one modern translation.**

3. **Mark your calendar.** Schedule daily time with God's Word.

4. **Keep an open attitude.** Bring no preconceived ideas to a passage. Ask God for new truths, insights, and challenges.

5. **Determine not to "dumb yourself down."** God's book *can* be understood.

6. **Establish a plan for reading the Bible through in a year.** The Bible can be read at a moderate rate in seventy hours. That translates into one hour and twenty minutes per week – sixteen minutes a day when reading five days a week, or eleven minutes if reading every day. Compared to the time we spend on other activities, Bible reading begins to look easy.[4] I chose a version that divides daily readings into portions from Old and New Testaments, *Psalms* and *Proverbs*. Such versions are available in Christian bookstores.

WHY READ GOD'S WORD?

From the following passages, personalize reasons you should feed upon God's Word. **Deuteronomy 8:3.** *Man does not live on bread alone but on every word that comes from the mouth of the LORD.*

Example: Just as bread is required for my physical growth, so feeding on the Word of God is necessary for spiritual growth.

Psalm 40:8: *I desire* _____.
Personalized: _____

Psalm 119:103: *How* _____.
Personalized: _____

Psalm 119:11: *I have hidden your word in my heart that* _____.
Personalized: _____

Jeremiah 15:16: *When your words came, I* _____
_____.
Personalized: _____

GOD VALUES HIS WORD

By matching the columns, complete God's statements about the value of His Word.

_____ **2 Timothy 3:16** | *All Scripture is God–breathed and* | **A** *but the Word of our God stands forever.*

_____ **Psalm 119:89** | *Your word, O LORD, is eternal;* | **B** *but my words will never pass away.*

_____ **Isaiah 40:8** | *The grass withers and the flowers fall,* | **C** *is useful for teaching, rebuking, correcting and training in righteousness.*

_____ **Matthew 24:35** | *Heaven and earth will pass away,* | **D** *it stands firm in the heavens.*

_____ **Matthew 5:18** | *I tell you the truth, until heaven and earth disappear,* | **E** *God will take away from him his share in the tree of life and in the holy city which are described in this book.*

_____ **Psalm 12:6** | *The words of the LORD are flawless,* | **F** *not the smallest letter, not the least stroke of a pen, will by any means disappear from the Law until everything is accomplished.*

_____ **Revelation 22:19** | *If anyone takes words away from this book of prophecy,* | **G** *like silver refined in a furnace of clay purified seven times.*

Answers: C, D, A, B, F, G, E.

DEVELOP A PLAN

While there are many plans for reading the Bible with understanding, here's my favorite. Adjust it to your needs.

Regard, Read, Record, Research, Reflect, Remember, Respond.

▶ **REGARD**. Seek God's face before hearing what He says in His Word. Have you ever talked to someone while he or she continued doing other things? Were you sure the person heard you? When someone speaks to you, do you pause to listen? God wants your full attention. Avoid listening to God while television or other things go on around you. Regard God with reverence as He speaks.

▶ **READ**. Choose short passages. Read aloud to receive God's Word the way a child receives – by hearing. Paul wrote, in **Romans 10:17**, *faith comes from*_____
_____.

▶ **RECORD**. Paraphrase briefly all that you remember from the passage. With practice you'll learn to listen more carefully as God speaks to you. His words flowing from your pen will register and remain in your mind.

▶ **RESEARCH**. For parts you need help in understanding, consult a commentary. There are many outstanding ones. Some are devotional by design while others are scholarly, offering comments by theologians and results of research. Compare several in a Christian bookstore or consult your pastor for guidance. Purchasing one volume at a time eases the cost.

A Bible dictionary is helpful, supplying pronunciations and meanings of unfamiliar words, where to find them in the Bible, and facts about biblical people, places, and things, including illustrations and maps. Compare before purchasing.

▶ **REFLECT**. We must meditate on a passage if we are to be "at one" with it. Reflect upon waking, before falling asleep, and at other times when you are alone. The psalmist described the ideal person in **Psalm 1:2**: *His delight is in the law of the LORD, and* _____
_____.

God said in Joshua 1:8, "*Do not let this Book of the Law*_____
_____ *written in it.*"

Place yourself in the story. Let God speak to you personally. For years I looked upon *The Bible* as a book *about* God, not realizing that God wanted to speak personally to me.

In reflecting, I use the acrostic, S–P–A–C–E: [5] Is there a(n):

Sin I should confess?

Promise to claim?

Attitude to adopt or change?

Command to obey?

Example to follow or avoid?

Watch for warnings, instruction, encouragement, comfort, or information that God imparts. Be alert for verses to claim as personal messages. For example, I reflect on Galatians 2:20 daily: *I have been crucified with Christ and I no longer live, but Christ lives in me.*

Is there a special verse you steer *your* life by? Record it here with the reference.

_____

_____

▶ **REMEMBER**. Memorizing Scripture helps us to think like God thinks. His concepts and values become ours when we have His Word hidden in our hearts.

• When noting a verse to memorize, read it in context – the passage(s) before and after – to understand its full meaning. First, write the reference (book, chapter, and verse), then the passage on an index card. Write the reference again following the verse. Sharing the reference proves God's authorship; listeners know you didn't originate the verse.

• To memorize, learn the reference, then the first phrase. Repeat it several times. Build on it by adding the second phrase, repeating it several times. Then quote the two phrases together several times. Continue this way until you learn the full passage, ending with the reference.

• My favorite way to memorize long passages is to record them for playback while I do housework or travel to and from appointments.

▶ **RESPOND.** Jesus asked a tough question in **Luke 6:46:** "*Why do you_____ _____?*" Responding is applying God's words in daily life.

Ask two questions while reading: *How do I apply this passage to my life today? and If I had been present, how would I have responded then?*

RESPOND

Lord, You have spoken to me in the following ways: _____

_____

_____

I confess the following sin (if any) Your Word has revealed in my life:

_____

_____

I respond by _____

Signature _____   Date_____

APPLY THE METHOD

1. REGARD. Seek God's face before listening to His Word.

2. READ. Matthew 13:1–9. The Parable of the Sower.

3. RECORD. Paraphrase and write down all you can remember.

Example: A farmer was scattering his seeds. Some fell on the hard path and birds ate them. Others fell on rocky places where the plants sprang up quickly, but because the soil was shallow, they couldn't develop deep roots. The sun scorched them and they died. Other seeds fell among thorns that choked the plants. Some seeds fell on good soil and produced a bountiful crop.

4. RESEARCH. You may need help from a commentary to understand the passage.

• For example, a parable is "an earthly story with a heavenly meaning," the handle for carrying a spiritual truth. The word "parable" (*parabole*) comes from the verb *paraballo,* "to cast alongside." Jesus taught in parables by casting an earthly story alongside a spiritual truth in order to give understanding to the latter.[6]

• In any parable, secondary truths are present, but the hearer is to determine one central truth. Discover it.

• The *"path"* (v. 4) was a roadway between rows left for travelers passing through the farmer's field. The soil became so hard that seeds couldn't penetrate and take root.

• Without research we might picture in verse 5 a field with lots of rocks, but with research we learn that in Palestine, much of the earth was a shallow covering over a shelf of limestone. Although seeds sprouted quickly, plants couldn't get root depth to find nourishment and moisture for withstanding the sun's heat. So they withered and died.

5. REFLECT. Meditate, relating the parable to your spiritual condition. Search your heart for ways the Gospel has fared in your life's soil.

• Verse 4. Is your soil hardened by the world's ways like the path of verse 4, so that God's Word can't flourish in your heart? ___ Yes ___ No

Claim Revelation 3:20.

_____

_____

• Is your soil "rocky" as in verse 5, due to priorities other than complete obedience to God? ___ Yes ___ No

Hear Luke 9:62. Jesus replied, "_____

_____."

• Is your life cluttered with "thorns," as in verse 7? Did you get your "ticket stamped for heaven," but hold to the clutter of materialism? Are you a fleshly Christian with one eye on things of heaven and the other eye on things of earth? ___ Yes ___ No

Write 1 Corinthians 3:13.

_____

_____

If you answered yes, list _"thorns"_ that choke your spiritual growth.

_____

How will you remove them in order to bear fruit for Christ?

_____

• Is your soil responsive like that of verse 8, producing a harvest proportionate to your ability? Is God's Word firmly rooted in your heart, controlling your desires, emotions, thoughts, and actions? ___ Yes ___ No

Write Galatians 6:9.

_____

_____

Read Matthew 25:14–30, noting that the reward was identical for all who bore fruit, regardless of their ability.

Write Jesus' words for you in verse 23: "_____

_____."

6. REMEMBER. Matthew 13:9: _He who has ears, let him hear. How many times did Jesus use some form of the verb "to hear" in Matthew 13?_

7. RESPOND. Pray, incorporating ideas gained from the Parable of the Sower:

• Seriousness of feeding upon God's Word

• Desire for the Gospel to bear fruit in your life (Matthew 7:16).

• Acknowledgment that all soils receive identical seeds from the same Sower

• The receptivity of the soil determines the outcome of the harvest

• Your responsibility for investing the Word sown in your life by others

• Thanksgiving for His love

Signature _____   Date _____

REFLECTING...

Following college graduation, Jack, then my fiancé, entered the Air Force. For two years he wrote to me daily. I read his love letters, re–read them, reflected on them, and remembered his words. Each day I responded.

On most days I also received some junk mail. If I opened it at all, I skimmed it and tossed it aside. Years later, alone at the ocean, I became convicted that I was treating God's love letter like junk mail. I devised a "meal plan" and began feeding myself regularly.

NOW WHAT?

You didn't enter the world feeding yourself. You were fed by others daily (not on Sundays only), until you could feed yourself. How often do you feed on God's Word?

___ Daily   ___ Almost daily   ___ When I'm in church   ___ Rarely

If your response was "rarely," who or what is feeding you?

___ Society ___ Church ___ Other_____

Who or what is feeding those closest to you?

___ Television   ___ Movies   ___ School   ___ Peers   ___ Other_____

I often joke, "A good meal is one that someone else prepared." In the spiritual sense, I enjoy being fed by sermons and Christian music, but I can't view them as my only food supply. If we grow spiritually, we must eat the spiritual food that is plentiful and available...*in all sixty–six books of the Bible!*

LEARNING TO DRESS YOURSELF

Put on the full armor of God, so that when the day of evil comes, you may be able to stand your ground, and after you have done everything, to stand.

— Ephesians 6:13

Read Ephesians 6:10–18.

When I was young, my mother laid out my clothes for school each day. Circumstances didn't find me dressed inappropriately because Mama foresaw my activities and prepared ahead. My responsibilities included taking up each piece of clothing and putting it on – fully, and in proper order.

Our heavenly Father, foreseeing our spiritual conflict, provides His armor to protect us when we're attacked by the world, the flesh, and the devil who stands ready to trip us up. Satan's very name, *Satanas* in Greek, means "one who resists." For spiritual combat, then, we are to *take up* God's armor and *put it on* – fully, and in precise order.

Can you even imagine a soldier going into a battle with no combat plan, carrying no weapon, and wearing no protective gear?

You and I are in God's army now. Let's get dressed for battle!

SPIRITUAL CHECK-UP

How often do you go *spiritually* streaking, dressed only in your *"helmet of salvation?"* (Ephesians 6:17)

___ Never. I'm always fully dressed.

___ Often. I have trouble looking "put together" spiritually.

___ What's that, again?

REFLECTING...

If ever I needed the full armor of God, it was when I returned to teaching following my years as a stay–at–home mom. Statistics that year were horrifying to me:

- ◗ Every 20 seconds, the life of an unborn baby was ended, averaging 4,000 daily.
- ◗ 20,860 babies and toddlers were abandoned.
- ◗ Pornography was a $32 billion–dollar business.
- ◗ Illegal drug sales topped $20 billion dollars.
- ◗ Homosexuality was an accepted life–style; fornication was called "sexually active," and adultery was casually referred to as "having multiple partners."
- ◗ Our nation began to regard God, and anyone standing for Him, as "the enemy." [1]

However, had you asked me, "Are you dressed for battle?" I would have responded, "*What battle?*" Naïve, I approached my work daily, unaware of Satan's strategy to disrupt my plans, destroy my joy, and dilute my spiritual influence on others, especially my teenaged students.

Before I became a Christian, Satan controlled me through my physical senses and my weak will to resist the world's pull. After I accepted Christ, my marriage to a minister sheltered me behind church walls. Now, having catapulted from home and church into the classroom, I landed full force on the battlefield of spiritual warfare, improperly dressed and defenseless in the face of an enemy attack.

Drug use was rampant in the school, and authorities struggled to deal with it. In addition, choral music (my subject) had become a course that students enrolled in for an "easy A." I had been hired to change chorus from a "sing–along" into a top performance group. With over fifty students in each class, I daily faced out–of–control youth expecting to do little to nothing instead of the hard work and precision that competitive choral music requires.

Many older students resisted with their "old natures" of former years' laxity. I found nails in my parking space; air released from my tires; gas siphoned from the gas tank; and someone threatened to put a pie in my face.

Despite these and worse incidents I can't relate, I remained ignorant of my struggle's true origin – until a student delivered a note from her mother. She wrote, "I pray for you daily because Satan doesn't want you in our school. He leaves the rest of us in charge of his demons, but he saves you for himself!"

Her message was a wake–up call from God: I was *not* struggling against flesh and blood. My enemy was Satan, and God used a caring Christian to enlighten me!

Unfortunately, society often absorbs and reflects Satan's ways. Joni Eareckson Tada said, "We live today in a world in which the thing that was once unthinkable becomes tolerable. And then acceptable. And then legal. And then applaudable."[2]

Christianity's dilemma is three–fold:

▶ Many new Christians fail to mature spiritually, and, not knowing God's Word, continue living by their earthly natures.

▶ Other Christians mistakenly believe that once they convert, their troubles will cease. As troubles continue, many begin to doubt their salvation and stop sharing their faith.

▶ Still others, ignorant of the spiritual struggle described in Ephesians 6:10–18, come under attack by Satan's "flaming arrows" (verse 16), and retreat. There's an old saying: "You can't beat age and experience." Satan has both.

WHAT ABOUT YOU?

Describe a time when you were frontally attacked by forces of evil.

_____

_____

_____

_____

_____

_____

How did you respond?

_____ I reacted in my own strength.

_____ I reflected Christ in the strength of *"his mighty power."*

Explain.

_____

_____

_____

_____

_____

_____

_____

SPIRITUAL WARFARE

In **Ephesians 6:10–18**, Paul unfolds a three–fold strategy: identify your enemy; devise a plan of resistance; and persevere.

IDENTIFY YOUR ENEMY

Many people don't believe Satan exists, but we have only to look within, at our personal surrenders to temptation, and to trace his tracks in the world through crime, sin, and disbelief.

1 John 2:16. *Everything in the world – the* _____

_____

_____

_____

Cravings: Addictions, sexual immorality, overeating

Lust of the eyes: Excessive desires: cars, clothes, jewelry, houses, furnishings

Boasting: Oversized appetites for financial gain, status, and power [3]

Many biblical scholars believe that Satan was Lucifer, described in Isaiah 14:12–15 as the angel God cast out of heaven because of his pride and intention to occupy God's throne.

I decided that where Satan originated was less important than where he intended to go in my life. For years I had equated him with God – goodness on one hand, evil on the other – with my fingers crossed, hoping God would triumph. Scripture taught, however, that Satan is a created being, neither eternal, all–knowing, all–powerful, nor all–present. He is, however, alive and active.

List his helpers named in Ephesians 6:12.

1._____ 2._____ 3._____

4. _____

In **1 Peter 5:8**, Peter described Satan's frontal attacks: *Your enemy* _____

_____

_____.

At other times, Satan works through sabotage, leaving us to accept blame for his schemes, or attach the blame to others.

Paul, in **2 Corinthians 10:3–4** wrote, *Though*_____

_____

_____

_____

_____

WHAT IS A STRONGHOLD?

A *stronghold* is a command post from which the enemy works in surrounding areas, and a place where Satan's thoughts seem more credible than our thoughts or God's. It's a system of logic – a lie used to carry out Satan's purposes in our lives. Strongholds exist in our minds, the church, and the environment. [4]

REFLECTING...

When I answered our doorbell, a woman stood on the porch weeping. I invited her in, and she shared her story. A friend had turned against her, accusing her of things she had neither said nor done. The two were members of a club where tensions between them affected the atmosphere of the entire group. Satan was using the woman's stronghold of accusation as a command post to shoot his flaming arrows at others.

I asked, "How would you prefer to settle this – man's way or God's way?"

She looked puzzled. "What do you mean?"

"This person has falsely accused you. You can condemn her and end the friendship. That's the fleshly way."

"Explain the other way," she said.

"You assume all or part of the blame. Jesus called it "turning the other cheek." Tell her you cherish her friendship, and you erred in some things you did and said. As a Christian, you will have to take the initiative, but you will heal the relationship and keep the friends you might otherwise lose because of her accusations."

"I prefer that way," she said. "You write the letter and I'll copy it."

After writing the letter I shared Christ with her. She recognized Satan's plan to isolate her from her friends and keep her bound in numerous strongholds.

I shared what I had painfully learned — we don't struggle with flesh and blood, but against spiritual forces of evil. She named several strongholds in her life, confessed them to God, and claimed Colossians 3:12, 14: *As God's chosen people … clothe yourselves with compassion, kindness, humility, gentleness and patience …. And over all these virtues put on*_____

_____.

By demolishing her strongholds, she clothed herself in righteousness, and restored her friendships. In time, not only did she renew her marriage by demolishing cold love, she also healed relationships with her daughters by demolishing failure and low self–esteem.

WHAT ABOUT YOU?

Having strongholds is not a shame, but keeping them is spiritually defeating. None of us is as free as Christ died to make us, or as free as we can be. The following list, compiled by Jack Taylor, identifies many strongholds Christians might unintentionally retain from their old natures.

As you read them, underline any you currently suffer from, remembering that occasional outbreaks are natural. It's only when they become rooted and compulsive that they become strongholds.

Hint: Saying, "I don't have any strongholds" is confessing at least one: Denial. :

General Categories:

Fixations, compulsions, obsessions, addictions, fears, anxieties, delusions, curses, some eating disorders, some sleeping disorders, prejudices.

Specific Problems:

Greed, anger, pride, bitterness, jealousy, lust, perversion, resentment, spite, laziness, negativism, pessimism, accusation, failure, perfectionism, irresponsibility, self–consciousness, vengefulness, grief, regret, love grown cold, condemnation, guilt, lying, confusion, deviousness, selfish ambition, suspicion.

These lists are not exhaustive, but will help in detecting strongholds.[5]

NOW WHAT?

How many did you underline? _____

Demolish them with the Word of God. For example, are you bound by fear? Claim 1 John 4:18: *Perfect love*_____

_____

_____

_____

Claim 2 Corinthians 10–5–6: *We demolish*_____

_____

_____

_____

ARE YOU READY?

Pray: Lord Jesus, You died to make me free, but I can't be free until my thought patterns are consistent with Yours. I want to mature spiritually by demolishing my strongholds one at a time. Your Word gives me the authority to confront and demolish anything that holds me captive. You tell me in John 8:32, *"You will know the truth, and_____."*

I claim Your power to be free. I confess the stronghold of_____
and claim Your promise that it is no more.
In Your name I pray. Amen.

Signature _____   Date _____

Describe a situation when you mistakenly attributed Satan's scheme to someone else.

_____

_____

_____

_____

_____

How would you respond differently if the incident occurred today?

_____

_____

_____

_____

_____

List strongholds you demolished during this lesson.

_____

_____

_____

_____

_____

What scriptures did you claim?

_____

_____

_____

_____

_____

THE CHRISTIAN'S STRATEGY

Ephesians 6:13 *Put on the full armor of God, so that when the day of evil comes,*_____

_____.

Sometimes our best response is to *stand*. An anonymous person wrote, "Let it be known on whose side you are. If there is any doubt, something is wrong."

During my first two years back in the classroom, I could only stand against the attacks from students who resented the new class structure. However, in the meantime, I invested great energy in building the new program through the incoming students. By the time the older students graduated, my influence, not the other teacher's, had become the foundation of the new program.

How many times in Ephesians 6:10–18 did Paul urge us to *stand*? _____
Under what circumstances have you stood recently for Christ?

_____

_____

_____

Name something from which you will never retreat.

_____

_____

_____

WHEN SHALL WE STAND?

Verse 13 *...when the day of evil comes...*

Check a *"day of evil"* you experienced recently:
___ Confusion, feeling that nothing I do turns out right
___ Depression over world conditions
___ Helplessness over personal problems
___ Feeling that God has forsaken me while blessing others
___ Feeling like an outcast at work
___ Suspecting murmurings behind my back
___ Other _____

These are examples of an enemy attack. When we blame God or others, Satan never has to take credit. Did you stand against the enemy at your "evil day"? ___ Yes ___ I'm afraid not

Explain.

_____

_____

THE ARMOR OF GOD[6]

Stand firm, I say:

Take salvation for helmet.

For coat of mail, put on righteousness.

Bucle on the belt of faith.

For sword, take that which the Spirit gives you – the words that come from God.

Let the shoes on your feet be the gospel of peace, to give you firm footing.

PUT ON THE FULL ARMOR OF GOD then you will be able to stand your ground against the schemes of the devil.

Take up the great shield of faith, with which you will be able to quench all the flaming arrows of the evil one, Ephesians 6:11–18
NEB

Paul undoubtedly observed the Roman soldiers who guarded him. He translated their armor into Christian terms, comparing it to qualities of character that distinguish the Christian. While the uniform is not the soldier, it does identify him.

God's armor is available, but we must *put on* each part. The Greek verb translated *"put on"* in verse 13 suggests urgent, decisive action: "Arm yourself."

While dressing physically, we begin with certain articles of clothing. We should put on God's armor in the correct order as well.

TRUTH

Ephesians 6:14 *Stand firm then, with*_____.
Paul indicated that being truthful is not a natural quality; honesty must be *put on.*

REFLECTING...

My mother died when tombstones with epitaphs were in style. My father had "A lover of truth" engraved on her tombstone.

If Jesus wrote your epitaph today, what do you hope He would write in regard to your honesty?

_____

Early Christians were noted for their honesty in a day when there was little regard for truth. Do you believe a person can still discern the difference between Christians and unbelievers by the way they handle the truth? ___Yes ___ No ___ Not sure

RIGHTEOUSNESS

Ephesians 6:14 *...with the breastplate of righteousness in place.*

The metal breastplate was vital in protecting the heart and lungs. Righteousness does this for the Christian. Our basic defense against evil is obedience to God's will and uprightness in conduct. Wrong attitudes and actions become weak spots in our armor through which the enemy can thrust his weapons. [7]

A Roman soldier could be spotted from a distance when his breastplate reflected the sun. What characteristic makes you recognizable as a Christian soldier?_____

How recently were you identified as a Christian?_____

Explain.

_____

_____

_____

_____

PEACE
Verse 15 ... *your feet*

The soldier wore sandals with hobnails in the soles to assure sound footing for battle. But the shoes have another meaning. They prepare and enable us to share the Gospel of peace with a lost world. The victorious Christian is a witnessing Christian, prepared with a thorough knowledge of the Word of God. [8]

What doctor would operate without a *"readiness"* from a qualified medical school? What unprepared engineer would be permitted to design buildings? When our shoes fit with the readiness of a knowledge of the Gospel, we have the *"beautiful feet"* described in **Isaiah 52:7**:

_____

_____

_____

FAITH
Verse 16 *In addition ... take up*_____

_____

The shield was four feet by two feet, made of wood, and covered with tough leather. It shielded the soldier's entire body, protecting him from spears and "flaming arrows" that were dipped in some flammable substance, ignited, and shot at the enemy. Satan shoots "flaming arrows" at our hearts and minds: lies, blasphemous thoughts, hateful thoughts about others, doubts, and desires for sin. Unless we quench these darts, they will light a fire within, causing us to disobey God. Not knowing when Satan will shoot a dart at us, we must walk using our shield of faith.[9]

Hebrews 11:1 defines faith: *Now faith is*_____

_____

_____

Have you committed your entire life in faith to God? ___ Yes ___ No

According to Ephesians 6:16, how many flaming arrows would your faith quench?
___ Some ___ Many ___ All

Which part of your life, if any, is not fully committed to God?

_____

_____

_____

If you answered the last question, why are you holding a portion of your life from the One who died for you? _____

SALVATION

Verse 17 *Take the* _____*of salvation*…. The helmet protects the head, our most vital and vulnerable part. Wearing it, we can rest, knowing that when our righteousness falters, our salvation remains intact. Our helmet of salvation cannot be removed, misplaced, lost, or stolen.

THE WORD OF GOD

Verse 17… *and the sword of the Spirit, which is*_____. The sword is our only offensive weapon. With it we can stand ready to attack as well as defend.

PERSEVERANCE IN PRAYER

Verse 18 Pray_____.

The hymnist urged, *Put on the gospel armor, each piece put on with prayer.* [10]

Prayer isn't part of the armor; it is the soldier's means of communicating with headquarters. Prayer is also the spirit with which the troops support one another. Paul urges prayer *for all the saints* (v. 18), indicating that the individual soldier isn't prepared until the entire army is ready.[11]

Perseverance requires remaining in God's Word so that His will is continually being done in our lives. Praying Scripture back to God keeps us anchored in Him, and assured that we are praying in His will.

I love praying Scripture and prayers I find in hymns. For example, I personalize the prayer of Habakkuk 3:17–19 whenever I'm discouraged:

Though it rains on my planned excursion, and a tire goes flat,

though some days I write long and produce little that is worthwhile,

though the savings dwindle and money runs short to pay bills,

yet I will rejoice in the Lord. I will be joyful in God my Savior.

The Sovereign Lord is my strength; he makes my feet like the feet of a deer.

Write one new truth you learned from **Ephesians 6:10–18**.

_____

_____

_____

_____

RESPOND

By praying Scripture you'll experience the oneness Jesus promised in John 14:20: "*I am in my Father, and_____.*"

Jesus taught His disciples that they "*should_____*"
(Luke 18:1), and Paul challenged us to "*pray_____*"
(1 Thessalonians 5:17).

We grieve God when we pray, "Lord, we come into Your presence," because we never leave His presence. (See Matthew 8:28.)

Evelyn Christenson wrote, "I think of praying unceasingly as turning the dial of my communication system with God to on, making possible a two–way conversation with Him at any time. That way, when I feel the fiery darts of Satan striking, communication with God is open and help is on the way." [12]

Finally, Paul requested prayer for himself (Ephesians 6:19). When did you last ask someone to pray for you?_____

When did someone last request that you pray on his or her behalf?_____

What does the person's confidence in your prayers mean to you?_____

NOW WHAT?

James 4:7 says: *Resist the devil, and* _____.

Notice that James says *resist*, not *attack*. While Satan has been defeated, check the ways you will resist him.

___ Stop my ears to his language

___ Shut my eyes to vulgarity

___ Judge my fleshly desires by God's Word

___ Protect myself with the shield of faith

___ Wield the sword, God's Word

___ Pray continually

What does God promise us for resisting Satan? (James 4:7)

_____

For how long? (See Luke 4:13.) *Until* _____

Whatever God is planning for you, your family, church, or city, it will no doubt involve engaging the enemy in warfare in order to accomplish God's will. But when we dress in God's *full* armor, we know that when the battle ends and the smoke clears, we'll be standing in possession of the field, ready for the next battle.

LESSON 7

BEARING THE FAMILY RESEMBLANCE

*We know that when he appears, we shall be like
him....*

— 1 John 3:2

REFLECTING...

Over lunch, Paula shared an incident about her oldest son who needed his baby picture for a class project.

She said, "You know how you take your first baby's picture every time he rolls over? Johnny had dozens of pictures to choose from. Our excitement aroused the middle son's interest."

"'Where are *my* baby pictures?' he asked.

"I hadn't taken as many pictures of Paul, but I found a considerable number, gathered some, and handed them to him. The problem arose when Patrick, my third son, asked, 'Where are *mine*?'"

Paula said, "I was so busy with the first two children that I took almost no pictures of our third baby. But you know how all babies in the same family look alike, so I grabbed some pictures of each of the other two and said, 'Here, Honey.'"

Paula's story reminded me of my own childhood, when I was often told how much I resembled my daddy. Someone said, "He can't deny fathering you; you're too much like him."

WHAT ABOUT YOU?

Whose physical features do yours resemble most?

_____

_____

_____

With which family members' personality or character traits do yours compare?

_____

_____

SPIRITUAL LOOK-ALIKES

We expect to inherit characteristics from our earthly ancestors. Likewise, our spiritual births enable us to manifest characteristics of the family of God with whom we share *spiritual* kinship. Paul insisted that we're *members of one body* (Colossians 3:15), and Peter claimed in 2 Peter 1:4 that we *participate in*_____.

Therefore, the more we grow spiritually, the more we resemble Christ and our spiritual siblings.

RECOGNIZED BY OUR "FRUIT"

Jesus discussed these common characteristics among spiritual siblings, saying, *"Every good tree_____"* (Matthew 7:17). Unfortunately, the *earthly nature* with which we are born vies for control of our lives, bringing unhappiness whenever we succumb to flesh and the world in opposition to God's will and purpose.

Jesus said, *"By_____"* (Matthew 7:20).

Which kind of fruit does Paul describe in Colossians 3:5, 8, and 9?_____

What are we to do with it? Does Paul indicate that we have control over our earthly natures?

_____

_____

Read Colossians 3:5, 8, and 9. List characteristics of the earthly nature.

Verse 5:_____

Verses 8–9:_____

In **Galatians 5:19–21,** Paul enlarges upon earthly nature's behavior. List sins <u>not</u> included in the Colossians passage.

_____

_____

What an ugly brood! Circle any you recognize in yourself.

PUTTING "BAD FRUIT" TO DEATH

ACTION	HELP

A: Acknowledge susceptibility to relapsing into old sinful natures.

1 Corinthians 10:12:

*So*_____

_____

_____

B. Believe in overcoming by the power of our new nature which is greater than that of our old nature (2 Corinthians 5:17).

1 Corinthians 10:13:

*But when you are*_____

_____

_____

C. Crucify the flesh daily.

Claim Galatians 2:20:

*I have been*_____

_____

_____

_____

_____

D. Depend upon God's power and strength, hour by hour, to overcome temptations of the flesh. Rely on 1 Peter 1:13–15.

Philippians 4:13:

I can do _____

_____

_____

E. Evaluate daily progress.

Philippians 2:13:

*It is*_____

_____

_____

_____

SPIRITUAL CHECK-UP

Does "bad fruit" continue to plague you since you became a Christian? You may have strongholds carried over from your sinful nature that must be pulled down in order for you to resemble Christ. (Review Lesson 6.)

What three ways listed in James 4:8 will help you resist the devil so he will flee?

_____

Can you accomplish this in your own strength?

____It's too much to ask.   ____ Not in my strength, but by God's grace.

____Since Christ has set me free, can't I live as I please? Answer: Write Galatians 5:13.

_____

_____

We can't serve one another in love by operating from a fleshly "do–it–yourself kit."

Claim Philippians 2:13: *It is*_____

_____

_____

Every Christian possesses the Holy Spirit. Galatians 4:6 says, *Because you are*_____

_____

However, Christians aren't automatically *controlled* by the Spirit. Paul scolded fleshly Christians in 1 Corinthians 3:1–3: *Brothers, I could not*_____

_____

_____. *You are still worldly.*

REFLECTING...

Once during my teaching career, the yearbook staff printed baby pictures of the faculty.

The students tried to recognize us from our pictures. Remarkably, many of us still looked the way we did as babies.

WHAT ABOUT YOU?

Do you resemble your *old nature's* picture more than you resemble Jesus with your *new nature?*

____ I look different now. ____ I look much the same as I did before accepting Christ.

Explain.

_____

_____

_____

BEARING "GOOD FRUIT"

Jesus challenged His followers in John 15:16–17. According to verse 8, how can we resemble Jesus? *This is*_____

_____

JESUS LOOK-ALIKES

Read **Galatians 5:22–23** where Paul described the fruit of the Spirit we are to produce in order to resemble the family of Christ. Paul wrote in Galatians 4:6, *Because* _____

_____*our hearts....*

By the indwelling Spirit, we are able to bear fruit of the Spirit that Paul defined in Galatians 5:22–23: *The*_____

_____

_____

All nine qualities of character are social in nature and can only be practiced in relation to other people.

Warren Weirsbe says that while it's possible for the old nature to *counterfeit* some of the Spirit's fruit, flesh can never produce the fruit. One main difference is that when the Spirit *produces* fruit, God, not man, gets the glory.[1]

LOVE

In Galatians 5:22–23, Paul placed love first, perhaps because it's the most powerful of all human emotions and enhances all other fruit of the Spirit.

Love is acting in another's best interest with no expectation of return. Regardless of how horrible circumstances of life become, love has a way of being there. We watch war or natural disasters reduce cities to ruins; then we discover love on the scene, nursing the wounded and rebuilding schools and hospitals. Love never gives up.

Perhaps the best description of love in all literature is 1 Corinthians 13. Notice how Paul compared love with both the *gifts* of the Spirit and the *fruit* of the Spirit.

LOVE AND SPIRITUAL GIFTS

Verse 1. *If I*_____.
What spiritual gift is to be exercised in love?_____

Verse 2. *If I*_____.
What four spiritual gifts are named or implied?_____

Verse 3. *If I*_____.
What gifts are surpassed by love?_____

LOVE AND THE FRUIT

Beginning with verse 4, Paul compared love with the *fruit* of the Spirit.

Verse 4. *Love is*_____
List fruit compared with love._____

Verse 5. *It is not*_____
What one fruit of the Spirit does this verse summarize?_____

Verse 6. *Love does not*_____
What fruit is implied?_____

Verse 7. *It always*_____
In this verse, what fruit does the repeated word always suggest?
_____ Faithfulness _____ Gentleness _____ Self–control

Verse 8. Which spiritual gifts will one day cease to exist?

_____

Verse 9. State the reason for their cessation.

_____
_____

SPIRITUAL CHECK-UP

Select one expression of love and describe how you used it recently toward someone other than your family, and the difference it made.

_____ I spoke gently in the presence of harshness

_____ I expressed kindness

_____ I shared sympathy with someone grieving

_____ I offered security to a child

_____ Other_____

My love made the following difference:

_____

_____

JESUS SAID...

John 15:12: *My command is this:*_____

HOW *DID* JESUS LOVE?

Read the entire passage, write the specified verse, and explain how Jesus showed love for others. In light of the passage, state how we can also *"love each other."*

EXAMPLE:

Read John 8:1–11. Write verse 11. *"Then neither do I condemn you," Jesus declared. "Go now and leave your life of sin."*

> **EXPLANATION:** Jesus showed love for an adulteress by rebuilding her self–esteem following condemnation of her by others.

> **RESPONSE:** We can love the sinner without endorsing the sin.

Read Matthew 8:1–4. Write verse 3.

_____

> **EXPLANATION:** Jesus _____

> **RESPONSE:** Our loving touch_____

Read Mark 10:13–16. Write verse 16.

_____

    EXPLANATION: Jesus _____

    RESPONSE: We, too, should_____

Read Luke 23:33–34. Write verse 34.

_____

    EXPLANATION: Jesus showed love by_____

    RESPONSE: We are to_____

Read John 11:1–44. Write verse 35.

_____

    EXPLANATION: Jesus _____

    RESPONSE: We show love by_____

Read Luke 19:1–10. Write verse 7.

_____

    EXPLANATION: Jesus dined with_____

    RESPONSE: Hospitality evangelism is very effective in_____

Read Luke 10:25–37. Write verse 33.

    EXPLANATION: Jesus described a true neighbor as_____

    RESPONSE: We can_____

WHAT DID JESUS' LOVE COST?

Write John 15:13.

_____

_____

REFLECTING...

I once heard a beautician belittle a man who left his wife with a "house full of children." After the woman had raised the children herself, he then "had the nerve" to come home. The beautician punctuated every word: "And that fool thing took him back!"

The customers gasped and took turns berating both man and woman. I remained silent, thinking, *What a love story! Her love survived all odds because she kept faith that one day he would return.*

Realizing I hadn't commented, the beautician leaned over with her hands on her knees, glared at me, and demanded, "Well, what do *you* think?"

Remembering Romans 5:8, I said, "Well, he seems good for nothing except the garbage can — much like you and me the day Jesus took us back at Calvary."

She literally screamed, "You mean you would take him back?"

"Wait," I said, "we're not talking about me. I don't know whether I would have had the grace she showed. I'm only saying that we, too, had strayed from God when Jesus died to redeem us."

The shop grew deathly quiet. Unknown to me, a woman had been listening from another room where she washed hair for all the operators. At my next visit, she said, "Quick, tell me what's wrong with my life. My husband won't go to church, my preacher can't stand me, and I despise myself!"

I asked if she were a Christian. She insisted she was and wanted to reach her husband for Christ. "I don't know what is wrong with your life," I said, "but I can tell you what was wrong with mine."

I explained three kinds of people the Bible describes: The person without Christ, (1 Corinthians 2:14), the worldly Christian attempting to live the spiritual life in the power of the flesh (1 Corinthians 3:1–3), and the Spirit–controlled Christian (1 Corinthians 2:15–16). I pulled out a little booklet that I am rarely without and gave it to her.[2]

Within weeks she was radiant with joy.

"The most wonderful things have happened!" she said. "My marriage is like new, my husband is going to church, and the pastor has stopped avoiding me."

At my next visit, I learned that she no longer worked there. I never saw her again.

WHAT ABOUT YOU?

Do you resemble Jesus in loving your _____ Challenging child _____ In–laws
_____ Contrary neighbor _____ Jealous coworker _____ Other _____

Do you believe God loves everybody? (See John 3:16 and Psalm 89:32–33.) _____
Write Jesus' words in John 13:35. "_____

_____."

How does God show His love? (Romans 5:8):

_____

_____

JOY: LOVE'S GLADNESS

Joy is an attitude that is not dependent upon circumstances, not affected by weather, nor hampered by moods. Dependent only upon the indwelling Holy Spirit, joy springs not from what others *do*, but from who we *are* in Christ. Joy isn't a thermometer that registers our spiritual temperature, but a thermostat that determines it.

JESUS SAID...

John 15:11: "*I have told you this so that* _____

_____."

WHAT ABOUT YOU?

Check all that apply:
_____ I take time to smell the roses. _____ I smile constantly. _____ People often ask what I'm so happy about. _____ People sometimes ask me what is wrong.

How does the Holy Spirit give you joy?

_____

PEACE: LOVE'S POISE

Peace is an at–oneness with God and people, the absence of hostility. Peace results from an inward harmony with God's will. More than the absence of turmoil, peace is tranquility and poise in the midst of unfavorable circumstances.

JESUS SAID...

John 14:27: "_____
_____."

Name times when Jesus demonstrated peace.

_____

WHAT ABOUT YOU?

What, if anything, robs your peace?
____ Unconfessed sin ____ Guilt ____ Anxiety
____ Fear that life is slipping by without fulfillment of dreams and goals
____ Conflict ____ Failed plans ____ Other

State how someone can find peace in one of the above circumstances.

_____

_____

Write Philippians 4:7.

_____

_____

PATIENCE: LOVE'S PERSEVERANCE

Patience is the capacity to tolerate a person or thing over a period of time without complaint. It's restraint in the midst of provocation.

Ruth Graham, wife of Billy Graham, once said she would like to have on her tombstone words she saw on a sign along a stretch of highway where construction was underway: "End of construction. Thank you for your patience."[3]

WHAT ABOUT YOU?

____ I can hang in there.

____ I stay with a task until it's finished.

____ I show impatience when waiting.

____ Instead of waiting for God or others, I go ahead and get things done.

GOD SAYS...

"Be patient." When?

Romans 12:12:_____

1 Peter 2:19:_____

2 Timothy 4:2:_____

With whom? 1 Thessalonians 5:14:_____

For whom? Psalm 37:7: _____

How? Colossians 3:12:_____

KINDNESS: LOVE'S COURTESY

Someone once described kindness as "love in action with velvet gloves on." Kindness involves time, energy, and interest in others. Kindness can be expensive when it requires inconvenience. Kindness is love looking for good in others. Kindness loves sinners for what they might become with God's guidance.

JESUS SAID...

Luke 6:31: "_____."

Describe a time when you fulfilled Leviticus 19:18.

_____

GOODNESS: LOVE'S CHARACTER

The word "good" evolved from "God," so to be good is to resemble God. Goodness isn't synonymous with sinlessness, however. In Greek, goodness means benevolence. Words beginning with "bene" relate to goodness, indicating that wealth accumulated in God's love, joy, and peace are poured out in active ministry upon our fellowmen.[4]

REFLECTING...

While I was growing up, an older friend was especially good to me in ways that my parents were unable to be. I asked her once how I could ever repay her. She answered, "You can't. Help someone else." When I think of goodness, her benevolence comes to mind.

WHAT ABOUT YOU?

Describe times when you benefited from another's goodness.

_____

_____

Describe ways you've benefited others.

_____

_____

FAITHFULNESS: LOVE'S LOYALTY

How do you apply the faithfulness stated in Joshua 24:15 in today's society?

_____

Faithfulness includes fidelity, trustworthiness, and reliability. Paul's thinking was that Christians should manifest themselves through faithful discharge of all duties and the honest handling of all things committed to them.[5] Does your life resemble Joshua's?_____

JESUS SAID...

In Matthew 25:14–30, Jesus commended the servants who invested the talents their master entrusted to them, saying, "*Well done,* _____

_____

_____!" (Matthew 25:21).

Jesus didn't commend success, but faithfulness, stressing the value He assigns to the smallest deed done in His name (vv. 35–40). How recently were you faithful? Explain.

_____

_____

GENTLENESS: LOVE'S NATURE

Have you watched people suffer unbearably, yet remain gentle? True gentleness isn't produced by will power; it comes from the Holy Spirit.

The world doesn't value gentleness. Instead, it personifies gentleness in the proverbial Caspar Milquetoast – spineless and without self–motivation. Yet, Jesus bequeathed the earth to the gentle. Not synonymous with humility, which brings rewards in heaven, gentleness fits us for happiness on earth. The New Testament offers three characteristics of gentleness:

- Submissive to God's will (Matthew 5:5; 11:29; 21:5)
- Teachable (James 1:21)
- Considerate (1 Corinthians 4:21; 2 Corinthians 10:1; Ephesians 4:2) [6]

JESUS SAID...

"Take_____

_____" (Matthew 11:29).

Centuries later, who claims more love – Herod or Jesus, whose throne was a cross?_____

What has proved more powerful, the Cross, or swords and guns of all the armies that have ever marched?_____

WHAT ABOUT YOU?

Check synonyms with gentleness that describe you:

____ Good–natured ____ Mild–mannered ____ Easy to get along with ____ Forbearing

____ Even–tempered ____ Tender–hearted ____ Sympathetic ____ Compassionate

____ Charitable ____ Peaceable ____ Noble ____ Kingly ____ Other _____

From your self–evaluation, could someone say that you resemble Christ?_____

SELF-CONTROL: LOVE'S CONSTRAINT

Christians are no longer slaves to *flesh*, which is sinful in human nature. Self–control is a fruit of the Spirit almost impossible to fake, because flesh never saw a sin it didn't like. Freedom in Christ doesn't permit free reign to one's impulses and desires. Even when something is lawful, Paul suggested, in 1 Corinthians 10:23, 31, three–way test:

1. Verse 23. Is it_____?   **2.** Is it_____?   **3.** Verse 31. Is it_____?

In Galatians 2:20, a good verse to memorize, Paul claimed to have crucified the flesh with its passions and desires.

REMEMBER...

▶ While it's possible for the old nature to *counterfeit* fruit of the Spirit, flesh can't produce it.

▶ Fruit grows from union with Christ, the Vine. When Spirit produces fruit, God receives glory. When flesh is at work, the person is inwardly proud and hopes for compliments. The Spirit's work is to make us more like Christ for the purpose of bringing Him glory, not receiving praise from people.[7]

▶ Fruit grows best in a climate cultivated in God's Word. Paul said in Galatians 5:26,

"_____."

▶ Fruit doesn't burst forth. It requires time to grow and ripen by being connected to the vine, which is Christ (John 15:1–8).

▶ Fruit of the Spirit is produced to be eaten, not admired. People starve for love, joy, peace, and all fruit of the Spirit. When they find it in our lives, they see in us something they lack.[8]

REFLECTING...

Jesus said, *"A tree is recognized by its fruit."*

Part of my college biology exam was to identify trees by their bark and leaves. I remember thinking, *If I could only see some fruit!*

I have sometimes wondered if God looks down and, seeing barrenness, cries, "If I could only see some *fruit!*"

RESPOND

Which fruit of the Spirit needs most attention in your spiritual growth? _____

Stay focused on Christ and He will produce it. Salvation is the beginning of Christian life, not the end. Jesus wants us to mature until the world notices our Family resemblance. Pray, personalizing Galatians 6:14 and Colossians 3:5. Conclude by praying Galatians 2:20.

_____

_____

_____

Signature _____ Date _____

ASSUMING YOUR ROLE IN THE FAMILY

From him the whole body, joined and held together by every supporting ligament, grows and builds itself up in love, as each part does its work.

— Ephesians 4:16

REFLECTING...

While our daughter Melanie was in labor, her dad and I made ourselves "small" in the coat closet of her hospital room. We wanted to be present to welcome this newborn with no past, only a future, into the family, without interfering with the process.

We were impressed with the amount of activity in the room as Nathanael inhaled his first breath from God. The doctor and nurses were trained and ready to assist this newborn in getting off to a healthy start in life. It would have been unthinkable for them to line up to shake the baby's hand and say, "Welcome to the world! Now, you're on your own."

The following Sunday, Jack and I were back home in the church he served as interim pastor. At the end of his sermon he invited people to unite with the church. A young woman named Janie responded. She had just breathed *spiritually* for the first time. She, too, was a new creation, with no past, only a future. (See 2 Corinthians 5:17.) At Jack's suggestion, Janie's new Christian family lined up, shook her hand, and welcomed her into the family.

Through physical eyes, church members often mistake adult new believers as being spiritually mature, or at least capable of growing by themselves. Because Janie was a physical adult, they didn't see her as the spiritual infant she was.

The weeks following found Janie regular in worship. But soon we noticed her attendance had become sporadic, until finally she stopped coming. Concerned and knowing how critical the months following a person's spiritual birth are, we kept in touch with her by telephone, notes, and quick visits. We encouraged her to join the new members' class, but she resisted. In time, she slipped through the cracks of the church, virtually unnoticed.

Months later, a church leader asked me whether I remembered a young woman – blond, in her mid–thirties, who once sat in the middle of the worship center during church. Looking befuddled, the church leader snapped her fingers, saying, "You know, what's her name?"

Janie had digressed from being her "new sister in Christ" to the anonymous "What's–Her–Name."

I compared Janie's spiritual birth to Nathanael's physical birth. How impossible it would have been for his excited siblings to ever address him as "What's–his–name." Instead, they hovered near, prepared to meet his every need. When he began to walk, they steadied him; picked him up when he fell; brushed him off and encouraged him to resume his walk.

Janie's Christian family, by their failure to further assimilate her, had told her, "From now on, you're on your own."

As a new Christian I, too, had once been part of that endangered species. Having joined a church that offered no help for new believers, I could easily have become a spiritual dropout … except for my romance with a soon–to–be preacher. The prospect of marrying Jack kept me in church, despite my slow spiritual growth. Joining the church choir and a Bible study group aided my assimilation.

Hopefully, you're in a church that maintains a heightened alert to the needs of new Christians. Holding this book indicates you're aware that establishing your role in a church family is a two–way proposition, that you share responsibilities for being assimilated.

YOUR RESPONSIBILITY

Check ideas that can speed a person's assimilation. Underline those you've practiced, or currently practice.

_____ Take the initiative and introduce myself to members, understanding that they've forgotten how it feels to be new.

_____ Attend every session of the new members' class.

_____ Refer to the church as _we, our,_ and _mine,_ not _they, their, and theirs._

_____ Visit several Bible study groups before choosing the one right for me.

____ Resist accepting service roles that would deny me opportunity for spiritual growth through Discipleship training and Bible study while I am young in my faith.

____ Mark activities in the church newsletter for my age group and participate in as many as possible.

____ Study the church's pictorial directory in order to put names with faces.

____ Attend church fellowships and meals, and mingle with different people each time.

____ Identify key leadership by attending church business sessions where I also learn and inquire about church polity.

THE CHURCH'S RESPONSIBILITY

To assimilate me into the church family, members should:

____ Introduce themselves until I can call their names.

____ Invite me to socials, offer rides or directions, and include me in conversation.

____ Stay in touch while I am new to the church.

____ Find ways to draw me into tasks or roles in the church.

____ Other_____

If you haven't experienced such efforts, review "Your Responsibility." Ask, "What more can *I* do to find my role in the church?" You might courteously suggest to the pastor that the church incorporate the above suggestions into means of helping new Christians become assimilated.

DISCOVERING YOUR ROLE THROUGH GIFTEDNESS

For a church to operate harmoniously, each member must contribute to it. Every Christian finds a path to service for God. Your natural talents and spiritual gifts provide avenues by which you can effectively serve the Body of Christ.

Write Romans 12:4–5.

_____

_____

TALENTS

At our natural births we received birthday gifts called talents. These talents are gifts from God that come to us genetically. As part of our physical natures, everyone, Christian or not, possesses inborn human traits and abilities. Perhaps you have your father's singing voice, your mother's sewing skills, or your grandmother's "green thumb."

Check your natural tendencies, naming ancestors who may have passed them on to you.
___ Athletic ___ Mechanical ___ Technical ___ Decorating ___ Sewing ___ Musical
___Woodworking ___Dramatic ___Artistic ___Agricultural ___Culinary ___Writing
___ Scientific ___ Other _____

I believe I received my _____ talent from _____ and
my _____ talent from _____
My present occupation in _____ may have resulted from inherited tendencies.

REFLECTING...

We differ not only in our number of talents but in their intensity. Some begin life with everything going for them, while others are born handicapped. However, every life is special and gifted by God to make a unique contribution to His world. God wants to use our inborn talents for His glory.

I was privileged to teach a handicapped girl who brought love and joy to everyone she met. Whenever she approached, I braced myself to receive a "bear" hug, and anticipated four hugs daily, at the start and end of piano lab and drama class. Meeting her in the hallway brought extra hugs. When the drama class presented Dickens' *A Christmas Carol,* I created a non–speaking role for her as one of the Cratchit children. Students and faculty noted and praised her performance.

SPIRITUAL GIFTS

When we were born again, we received spiritual birthday gifts from the Holy Spirit, Who began His formal earthly ministry when Jesus ascended to heaven following His resurrection.

Write Acts 2:33._____
_____

The word for *gifts* is derived from the Greek word for "grace." Gifts are "gracelets," granted by divine favor, <u>not</u> on the basis of spiritual performance or prominence. They are given not earned; bestowed not bought; conferred not sought. They are in the possession of the Spirit who distributes them as He wills. Please remember that God does not just give gifts; He gives the

Spirit who *possesses* the gifts. If you cannot understand your gifts, accept and use them anyway. Spiritual gifts are neither talents nor highly developed human abilities. They are spiritual, unseen, and real.[1]

Read 1 Corinthians 12:1–11. Answer, including the verses.

Verse 7. To which Christians are spiritual gifts given?_____

Who decides how spiritual gifts are distributed?_____

For what purpose are they given?_____

Read Romans 11:29–32. Answer, stating verses.

If we fail to use our gifts, will God take them back?

_____

_____

Why?_____

Below, the nine primary gifts found in 1 Corinthians 12:8–11 are listed with their meanings.

Wisdom	God–given insight into spiritual truth
Knowledge	The ability to know what is on God's mind and apply it to a given subject
Faith	The God–given ability to believe things about which the Bible is silent
Gifts of Healing	The supernatural intervention of God through a person to restore health to a body
Miracles	The God–given ability to accomplish beyond the normal range of the natural
Prophecy	God–given ability to speak God's Word in a known language
Distinguishing between spirits	The God–given ability to judge accurately the false from the true
Speaking in tongues	The God–given ability to speak in a language not known to the speaker
Interpretation of tongues	The God–given ability to translate an unknown language into an understandable message

Read Ephesians 4:12–13. Complete the three sentences, explaining ways in which spiritual gifts function:

1. They prepare God's people for _____.

2. They build up the Body of Christ until we all reach_____

_____

3. They help us become "*mature, attaining to* _____

_____."

From our point of view, spiritual gifts are gateways from the physical (natural) into the spiritual (supernatural). From God's point of view, they are gateways from the realm of the spirit into the natural. Our gifts, then, are avenues for allowing God's power to gain entry into our lives. Since Jesus promised this power, why wouldn't we expect Him to deliver the power promised to us to operate within our spiritual gifts? [2]

List the spiritual gifts in Ephesians 4:11.

_____

_____

From **Ephesians 4:14–15**, what results from using our gifts?

1. We will no longer be spiritual_____

2. We will in all things_____

Because Paul wrote to lay Christians in Ephesus, may we assume that God never intended for the Church to leave God's work to a small corps of professional clergymen?

THE MOTIVATIONAL GIFTS

Write Romans 12:6.

_____

Paul listed spiritual gifts in three passages: Romans 12:6–8, 1 Corinthians 12:8–10, and Ephesians 4:11. Those listed in Romans 12: 6–8 are sometimes called "motivational gifts." While Paul said you have at least one, it is possible to possess all seven.

The gifts below are taken from Romans 12:6–8. Study them and check those that describe you and motivate you to serve in Christ's Body, the Church.

1. Prophesying (Preaching).

The English word *prophecy* is derived from the Greek word meaning "public expounder." It has two meanings: first, the foretelling or predictive prophecy, which exists in rare instances today; second, according to 1 Corinthians 14:3, the edification, instruction, and exhortation of believers in a local congregation. [3]

_____ I feel compelled to speak for God. I am open and persuasive. I live according to what I proclaim. I will stand alone for what I believe is consistent with the Word of God.

Personal Scriptures:

2 Timothy 4:2. *Preach the Word; be*_____

_____

1 Corinthians 9:16._____

_____

Also see Acts 20:20–21; Acts 21:9; Ephesians 6:19.

If your motivational gift is prophesying (preaching), _____ according to Romans 12:6, how are you to use this gift?

_____

2. Serving (Helps).

I don't need recognition or even appreciation for serving anywhere I see or sense a real need. I invest my talents in the life and ministry of other members of the Body to enable them to increase the effectiveness of their own spiritual gifts.

Personal Scriptures:

Luke 22:26: *Instead,*_____

_____

Also see Matthew 25:23; Romans 16:1–2; Acts 9:36.

If helping motivates you, describe a recent experience when someone thanked you for your helpfulness. _____

3. Teaching.

I have the ability to illustrate and apply Bible truths to life. I uphold the truth and authority of the Scriptures. I enjoy studying and doing research to get facts. I can teach truth in the face of opposition when I must.

Personal Scriptures:

Titus 2:7–8: *In your teaching show*_____

_____

_____

Colossians 3:16: *Let* _____

_____*wisdom....”*

4. Encouraging. I urge Christians to grow in Christ. I welcome opportunities to counsel, and warn them when I observe behavior that is contrary to Christ's commands. I'm comfortable sharing words of consolation and encouragement to members of the Church in ways to make them feel they've been helped.

Personal Scriptures:
Ephesians 4:29: *Do not*_____

_____

_____

Also see Proverbs 12:25; Acts 14:22.

5. Giving. I often share with others, even when it means sacrificing in order to give. I find fulfillment supporting others' ministries, and I discern needs that could be helped by my giving. I give out of love, not duty. I enjoy giving to worthwhile causes where my identity is unknown.

Personal Scriptures:
Hebrews 13:16: *And do not*_____

_____

Also see Matthew 6:1–4; Luke 11:41; Deuteronomy 15:7–8; 2 Corinthians 8:2–5; 2 Corinthians 9:2, 6–8; Galatians 2:10.

If you're spiritually motivated to give, according to Romans 12:8, how are you to give?

_____

Describe a recent incident that confirmed your gift.

_____

6. Leadership. I have the ability to organize projects with final results in view. I recognize abilities in others, delegate responsibilities, and motivate others to work together harmoniously to accomplish goals for God's glory.

Personal Scriptures:
Hebrews 13:7: *Remember* _____

_____

Also see Ephesians 4:11; 1 Timothy 5:17; Galatians 6:1–2.

If you're motivated in leadership, according to Romans 12:8, how are you to govern?

_____

7. Mercy. I'm drawn to people in trouble, both Christian and non–Christian, and have a strong desire to help alleviate their suffering and supply their needs. I translate my compassion into deeds that reflect Christ's love. I avoid actions or words that would hurt others.

Personal Scriptures:

Luke   **10:33–35:**   *A*
*Samaritan,*_____

_____

Matthew 5:7: *Blessed*_____

Also see Acts 16:33; Mark 9:41; Romans 12:8.

If you're spiritually gifted with mercy, according to Romans 12:8, how are you to show mercy?

_____

List your motivational gifts.

_____

Describe recent experiences that validate your gifts.

_____

_____

Circle any you discovered that surprised you.

WAYS TO DISCOVER YOUR GIFTS

> *I remind you to fan into flame the gift of God, which is in you....*
> —2 Timothy 1:6

▶ Agree that the Holy Spirit has given you at least one spiritual gift and wants you to discover and use it to build up Christ's Body, the Church.

▶ Ask God to guide you in discovering your spiritual gifts. Follow Paul's advice in 2 Timothy 1:6.

▶ If you fear what God might call you to do with your gifts, confront your fear and confess it to God now.

▶ Try a variety of ministries and discover what you are best suited for in God's service.

▶ Listen when other Christians affirm your giftedness.

▶ As you mature in Christ and face new opportunities and challenges, you may discover dormant gifts emerging. Review 2 Timothy 1:6.

WAYS WE RESPOND

1. Use our gifts for building up the Church.
2. Abuse our gifts by using them for self–glory.
3. Refuse our gifts, thus quenching the Spirit who bestowed them. Paul warned in 1 Thessalonians 5:19, "*Do not*_____."

REFLECTING...

Years ago I searched for a house–warming gift for a special friend.

On visits to her home I had noticed that she didn't have a bedside clock. I found one that was the perfect size, in wood like her furniture. It came in a distinctive gift box, matching her impeccable taste.

As she opened the gift, no expression registered on her face. Without touching the clock, she closed the box, shifting her attention to other gifts. During later visits to her home, I never saw the clock displayed.

Years later an event arose in my life when a gift from her was appropriate. As I opened the box, there lay the clock, just as I had given it to her. Wounding me was not her motive; our friendship was too deep. As years passed, she had simply forgotten who gave it to her.

I held the clock and prayed, "Lord, have I refused *Your* gift? Have I said, 'This isn't the gift I wanted; give it to someone else?' By refusing Your gift, have I grieved your Spirit? Lord, give me additional time to stir up the gift that's in me, to glorify You through its use in building up the Church, and making an eternal difference in the world that Jesus died to save." AMEN.

WHAT ABOUT YOU?

▶ Since joining _____ Church, I've found my role in the church family by discovering and using my gift(s) of _____.

▶ During this lesson, I've discovered my spiritual gift(s) of _____ to use in building up the Body of Christ.

NOW WHAT?

Just as we didn't enter the physical world fully grown, neither did we become spiritually mature the moment we received Christ as Savior. Salvation is only the beginning of the Christian life.

You've heard the well–worn cliché: "God isn't finished with me yet." There's much truth in that. As Christians, we're to be constantly growing, both by the Word of God and by exercising our spiritual gifts in order to impact the world for Christ.

RESPOND

Pray, thanking God for both your natural talents and spiritual gifts. Ask the Holy Spirit to guide you in using them for the good of the Church. Thank Him for making you a unique part of the Body of Christ, and thank Him for your spiritual siblings around the world whom you will meet in heaven … *with their gifts on full display.*

LESSON 9

LEARNING THE FAMILY RULES

Why do you call me, "Lord, Lord," and do not do what I say?

— Luke 6:46

REFLECTING...

"Mama, is that in the Bible?" We often teased our mother when her one–liners rang from the kitchen.

"Well, if it isn't, it ought to be!" she would joke, unruffled by our attempt to distract her from teaching us how to live. Her "speech is silver, but silence is gold" halted many conversations she feared were getting out of hand. She often quoted the Bible, as if expecting to see its words lived out through us.

While we learned obedience, we never achieved God's standards. Surely, Mama knew we wouldn't, being as familiar with our inherent weaknesses as with her own. Still, she never lowered the bar of her expectations. Instead, she defended her stance, claiming, "Times may have changed, but God has not!"

In terms of obedience, we characterize children today as strong–willed or compliant. By nature, I was compliant, relishing approval, until as a teenager I began testing the grip of my parents' reins, especially when their rules seemed designed to squeeze the fun out of life.

When they forbade my going places, I often whined, "Everyone else will be there!"

My unimpressed father would answer, "That may be a good reason for your *not* going!"

In answer to my *"Why?"* he would say, "Look at me. The reason is, 'Because I said so.'" My parents' unwavering *"You may"* or *"You may not"* settled matters quickly and finally.

Later, I discovered their parenting style was much like God's. In delivering the *Ten Commandments,* God spoke in absolutes: *"You shall; you shall not."* Instead of pleading, "Please choose Me over other gods," He stated emphatically, *"You shall have no other gods before me"* (Exodus 20:3).

When people complain, "But, there's truth in *all* religions!" God responds, "Read My Word. Bring your life into compliance with it. No further comment!" Jesus echoes, *"Why do you call me 'Lord, Lord,' and do not do what I say?"* (Luke 6:46).

WHAT ABOUT YOU?

Was obedience to your parents or guardians non–negotiable? ___ Yes ___ No ___ Sometimes

Which of the following reflected your attitude toward their commands?
___I felt made to comply. ___ I felt privileged to comply. ___ Comply? Not me.

How did your attitude toward obeying your parents or guardians affect your willingness or reluctance to obey God's commands later in life?

_____

_____

Name the following Bible characters. Define their circumstances and the attitudes with which they obeyed God's call.

SCRIPTURE	CHARACTER	CIRCUMSTANCES OF GOD'S CALL	ATTITUDE STRONG–WILLED OR COMPLIANT
Example: *Genesis 17:23*	*Abraham*	*To circumcise himself and all males in his household*	*Compliant*
Exodus 4:13–20 _____		_____ _____	_____
Judges 6:14–29 _____		_____ _____	_____
Jeremiah 1:4–17 _____		_____ _____	_____
Jonah 1:1–3; 3:3 _____		_____ _____	_____

Luke 1:26–38 _____ _____ _____

_____

John 17:4 _____ _____ _____

_____

JESUS, OUR EXAMPLE

IN CHILDHOOD

Luke 2:51: *He went down to Nazareth with them* [Mary and Joseph] *and*_____

_____*to them....*

IN ADULTHOOD

Philippians 2:8: *Being found in appearance as a man, he*_____

_____

WHAT ABOUT YOU?

Recall a time when you resisted God's command, but reconsidered, and obeyed.

_____

Once you submitted to God's will, how was your strong will used to God's advantage?

_____

Describe a recent time when you heard God's command through Scripture, sermon, or some other means, and obeyed.

_____

_____

How did your prompt compliance with God's command prove helpful?

_____

THE TEN LAWS

The *Ten Commandments* given in Exodus 20:1–17 remain as vital today as when the Israelites gathered thousands of years ago to hear Moses recite the words he received from God on Mount Sinai. No single document has so influenced civil law in western nations as have these ten edicts.

During 400 years in Egyptian slavery, the Israelites' ancestors had lived in an idolatrous environment, and the mark of that experience remained on them. Now they were about to enter the Promised Land and form a nation that would be surrounded by peoples who worshiped many gods.

So, with ringing authority, God began, *"I am the Lord your God."*

It is as if He said, "When you worship other gods, sow seeds of wickedness, and reap bitterly what you sowed, I will still be your God, faithful to you and unchanging."

We should remember that the *Ten Commandments*, like Jesus' *Sermon on the Mount,* were addressed to redeemed people. They cannot be broken. We can only break ourselves *on* them, courting certain disaster.

I sometimes hear unbelievers say, "I just live by *The Sermon on the Mount,*" as if Christ's highest standards were their starting point, when the only possible point of beginning is salvation in Christ. Without a new birth and a new spirit, one cannot live by the same standards of those redeemed by Christ on the Cross.

Choose one definition of Christian conversion:
____ Living by the *Ten Commandments*
____ Surrendering to Christ as one's personal savior
____ Agreeing with historical facts about Jesus

WHAT ABOUT GRACE?

We hear the arguments, "Christians live under grace, rather than under the Law" and "Aren't Christians required to obey the Ten Commandments?" Both are true. However, this doesn't place the Law above grace. (See Ephesians 2:8–9.)

On one occasion, recorded in Matthew 5:17–20, Jesus insisted that:
1. He had *not* come to *abolish*_____.
2. He came, instead, *to*_____.
3. According to verse 19, *anyone who breaks one of the least of these commandments, and teaches others to do the same will be called*_____
*but whoever practices and teaches these commands will be called*_____.

WHAT ABOUT YOU?

Based on your present obedience to God's commands, what might you be called in heaven today?

_____

God made His commands in Hebrew to the second person singular voice, meaning to you personally. Place your name in every commandment, acknowledging that God holds you responsible for obedience to the Law. Look for ways to bring your life more in line with God's expectations.[1]

JESUS' TEACHINGS AND THE LAW

In addressing the Israelites, God was concerned with their outward behavior. Jesus went further, including the inner desire that _leads_ to behavior, spotlighting the difference between action and desire. Where God commanded, "Do not murder," Jesus said, "Do not get angry, because anger _leads_ to murder."

With which of the following do you agree?
_____ Actions are controlled more easily than thoughts.
_____ The world judges outward behavior, while God looks upon the heart.
_____ Growing spiritually is a daily struggle between our physical and spiritual natures.

ONE

GOD SAID...

You shall have no other gods before me (Exodus 20:3)

JESUS SAID...

"No one can serve two masters. Either he will hate the one and love the other, or he will be devoted to the one and despise the other." (Matthew 6:24.)

We should wonder, "How could any god remain worthy of worship if he were willing to step aside to allow "other gods" to reign in our lives for a time?"

WHAT ABOUT YOU?

Everyone serves a god. What "other gods" attempt to infringe upon your loyalty to God?

____ Self ____ Work ____ Position ____ Popularity ____ Beauty ____ Fame

____ Materialism ____ Knowledge ____ Pleasure ____ Sports ____ Institutionalism

____ Drugs ____ Lust ____ Philosophy ____ Secularism ____ Other _____

Can any of the above save, heal, bring you through the shadow of death, or defend you in the judgment? _____

Joshua 24:15 says, *"If serving the Lord seems undesirable to you, then choose for yourselves this day whom you will serve.... But as for me and my household,_____."*

Do you stand today with Joshua? Explain.

_____

_____

TWO

GOD SAID...

*You shall not make for yourself an idol in the form of anything in heaven above
or on the earth beneath or in the waters below (Exodus 20:4).*

Today we no longer carve gods from wood, but this commandment still holds meaning. We must be certain we never allow our focus to shift from God to an object or image meant only as a symbolic reminder of God. Yet an idol isn't just an image of an inanimate object or something we envision. Anything can become an idol when it interferes with our relationship with God. While several obvious things might come to mind, we must realize that career, money, materialism, hobbies, sports, knowledge, and even family can become idols when they become all encompassing, a substitute for His presence, or a substitute for spending time in His presence.

In Exodus 20:5, what reason did God give in forbidding the making of idols?
" _____."

JESUS SAID...

"God is spirit, and his worshipers must worship in spirit and in truth" (John 4:24).

One day a Samaritan woman engaged Jesus in discussion over the location of the true place of worship. She said that while Jews taught that one must worship in Jerusalem, her ancestors taught that the true place of worship was Mt. Gerizim. Jesus declared that it was not where one worshiped, but how one worshiped that was important – *in spirit and in truth*. The true worship of God is in one's heart. [2]

REFLECTING...

Even rituals can become idols. My husband Jack once substituted several weeks at a church during the pastor's illness. The church met in assembly before dividing into study groups. Without exception, each week the assembly leader followed a ritual: He led the group in two hymns, read Scripture, prayed, led a third hymn, and dismissed the group to their classes.

One Sunday the leader was away. Feeling bold enough to experiment, Jack suggested that the substitute direct only one hymn and ask the group to be seated. The young man went along with the suggestion, and following the first hymn, said, "Be seated."

No one sat. Instead, they looked at each other as if hoping someone would correct this fellow who had not observed their pattern of singing *two* hymns before sitting. The group finally, and awkwardly, sat after the substitute began reading Scripture.

WHAT ABOUT YOU?

Check "idols" you have observed. Underline any you regretfully have participated in.

____ The Lord's Prayer being "recited" without giving thought to its meaning

____ Plastic images on dashboards – or jewelry being worn – for protection

____ Teenagers using church as an excuse to drive the car

____ People moving their church membership when the pastor accepts a new call

____ Churches clinging to outdated buildings for sentimental ties to the past

Every heart hungers for God. Idol worship is a meager attempt to fill that longing for the true God.

THREE

GOD SAID...

Exodus 20:7

_____

_____

We don't like seeing our names misspelled, or hearing them mispronounced, because our names represent all we are and all we stand for. God's name is above all names and deserving of our reverence and respect.

JESUS SAID...

Matthew 12:36–37: *"I tell you that men will have to give account on the day of judgment for*

_____

_____*."*

WHAT ABOUT YOU?

Check ways God's name is misused. Underline those you feel a need to guard against.

_____ Claiming the name *Christian* without being saved

_____ Using His name in profanity

_____ Referring to God irreverently, such as "The Man Upstairs"

_____ Failing to take His Word seriously

_____ Slipping references to God into speeches for political purposes

_____ Joining a church for business reasons, to "cash in" on God's name

RESPOND

Pray, asking God's forgiveness for times, if any, when you find yourself misusing His name. Promise to guard the use of His name in the future. Intercede for others who use His name inappropriately.

FOUR

GOD SAID...

Remember the Sabbath day by keeping it holy (Exodus 20:8).

Genesis 2:2–3: *By the seventh day God had finished the work he had been doing.... And God blessed   the   seventh   day   and   made   it   holy, because*_____

_____

God said, *"Remember,"* as if He expected us to forget. We can forget two ways: intentionally, and by crowding our minds and calendars with other activities.

REFLECTING...

As teenagers, my date and I often drove to a nearby city on Sunday evenings to people–watch and window–shop. The windows in one department store were noticeably different; black curtains concealed the merchandise. The owner was determined to keep the Lord's Day holy by refusing people even the *desire* to shop at his store on Sundays.

Today many people see Sundays as any other day. This is sad, because God established a rhythm of work and rest, providing a day to relax, reflect, and worship in the midst of ongoing life. Additionally, all time belongs to God, and this special day out of seven reminds us of the sacredness of all our days.[4]

JESUS SAID...

*"The Sabbath was made*_____

_____*"* (Mark 2:27).

Luke 4:16 adds, *"On the Sabbath day he*_____

_____*."*

Jesus healed and led people to God on the Sabbath, proving that, while He is the Son of God, He was also His brother's keeper. We assume then that we are not to sit with folded hands on

Sunday. Because of work schedules, many Christians attend churches that offer worship opportunities on days other than Sunday. Early Jewish Christians changed their day of worship from the last day of the week, the Jewish Sabbath, to the first day of the week (which later became knows as Sunday), for two reasons. First, it was the day Jesus rose from the grave. Second, they didn't want their meetings to be confused with Jewish worship services. They were celebrating the resurrection of the Messiah. The Sabbath commemorates God's rest following His work of creation. The Hebrew word *Sabbath* means "to cease" or "to rest." [5]

Instead of asking, then, "Is there anything wrong with what I do on Sunday?" ask, "Am I doing the highest possible *good*?"

Complete the following guidelines for the Lord's Day observance.

Colossians 3:2: "*Set your minds on*_____."

Hebrews 10:25: "*Let us not*_____,

_____."

WHAT ABOUT YOU?

1. Describe your typical Lord's Day activities.

_____

_____

2. Check ideas you agree with.

The Lord's Day is for:

_____ Worship and praise _____ Rest _____ Change of pace

_____ Family togetherness _____ Self–examination _____ Other _____

Do your answers in #2 match your description in #1?

_____

If not, how can you make the two agree?

_____

3. Judge your activities.

Would Jesus do what I normally do on the Lord's Day?

_____

Do my activities honor Him?

_____

_____

Would I invite Jesus to come along? Why or why not?

FIVE

GOD SAID...

Honor your father and your mother, so that you may live long in the land the LORD your God is giving you (Exodus 20:12).

This is the only commandment with a promise, implying that parents or guardians are representatives of God. The way we honor them indicates our concept of God. This places great responsibility on parents. A parent who betrays a child's trust has undermined God's relationship with the child. [6]

JESUS' EXAMPLE

He went down to Nazareth with them and was obedient to them... (Luke 2:51).

Jesus' submissiveness showed that children are not to grow up flouting parental rules. If allowed to, they may flout national laws when they are older.

This commandment is not limited to children; it includes adults. During childhood, we *obey* our parents. As adults, we *honor* them with the dignity and respect God says they deserve.

Society does not always deal well with aging parents. We have worshiped at the shrine of youth for a long time, but those who build a society in which old age is honored may expect to enjoy similar treatment in their later years.[7]

WHAT ABOUT YOU?

Of all living creatures, the human being experiences the longest dependency on others.

Check reasons for honoring your parents or guardians.

____ They gave me life.

____ They provided protection, food, and clothes when I was helpless.

_____ They experienced life first and advised me of its pitfalls.

_____ Other_____

Choose one of the statements above. Write a paragraph describing a recent time when you honored your parents or guardians.

_____

_____

If they are already in eternity, give thanks for their influence.

_____

If you are unable to honor your parents' beliefs or behavior, thank God for their giving you life.

_____

_____

SIX

GOD SAID...

You shall not murder (Exodus 20:13).

William Barclay insists that this command does not eliminate capital punishment or killing during war, because the same chapter (Exodus 20) and the following chapter (21) list crimes punishable by death. What _is_ forbidden is the reckless life of anger, violence, bitterness, or any selfish purpose, such as robbery. [8]

JESUS SAID...

"You have heard that it was said..., 'Do not murder...' But I tell you that anyone who is_____ _____" (Matthew 5:21–22).

The question of whether a Christian goes to war is not answered here. On one hand, Christians cannot observe rampant evil and leave it unchecked. The Bible includes many accounts of God ordering His people to kill their enemies.

On the other hand, Jesus taught us to love our enemies, and we cannot love people by killing them. He could have blasted His own enemies out of existence; instead He chose the Cross. It's best to leave this issue to each individual's conscience, and respect each other's choices. [9]

WHAT ABOUT YOU?

Check passive ways one can "kill." Underline those you regretfully engaged in without realizing their severity.

_____ Gossiping

_____ Destroying someone's reputation by bearing false witness in court

_____ Targeting another person with continual and excessive anger

_____ Dealing in illegal drugs

_____ Employing people to work in known unsafe environments

_____ Other_____

SEVEN

GOD SAID...

You shall not commit adultery (Exodus 20:14).

Adultery is sexual intercourse with a married person; fornication is sexual intercourse before marriage. Scripture condemns both. (See Matthew 15:19 and Acts 15:20.) In 1 Corinthians 6:13, Paul insisted, "*The body is not meant for sexual immorality, but*_____

_____."

JESUS SAID...

"*You have heard that it was said, 'Do not commit adultery.' But I tell you that anyone who looks at a woman lustfully has already committed adultery with her in his heart*" (Matthew 5:27–28).

The hallmark of a Christian is self–control, a characteristic separating us from animals. Allowing sexual passions to master us is animal–like. Scripture insists on sexual purity. First Corinthians 6:18 warns, "_____."

Colossians 3:5–6 lists five things that belong to our earthly nature that should be put to death now that we are Christians. Name them._____

According to Paul, we all once walked in these ways, but now we must rid ourselves of such things because we have taken off the old self and put on the new self which "*is being renewed in*_____" (vv. 9–10).

WHAT ABOUT YOU?

Answer True or False to statements concerning your personal beliefs.

____ My body belongs to God.

____ Self–control is a test of a Christian.

____ Sex before marriage degrades a person made in God's image.

____ True love never harms another person.

____ Having sexual intercourse before marriage is claiming privilege without responsibility.

____ Sexual intercourse should be the consummation of marriage between a man and woman.

EIGHT

GOD SAID...

You shall not steal (Exodus 20:15).

JESUS SAID...

"A man was going down from Jerusalem to Jericho, when he fell into the hands of robbers. They _____" (Luke 10:30).

This was an example of active stealing, the sin of commission. But in verses 31–32, Jesus made it clear that one can also sin by omission: What two individuals in His story *"passed by on the other side"* when we would have expected them to help the wounded man?

_____

We label what they did as "passive" stealing because while they didn't finish him off by driving their chariots over him when they passed by him, they did deny him the help he needed.

Passive stealing is cunning and dangerous because it relieves us of guilt, making repentance impossible.

WHAT ABOUT YOU?

Recall a recent time when you were so busy doing "good things" that you passed by someone in need.

_____

Describe a time when were you in need of help and others passed *you* by.

_____

Check activities you would label passive stealing.

_____ Taking advantage of a weaker person in a financial deal

_____ Accepting welfare while able to support oneself

_____ Failing to report full earnings to the government

_____ Borrowing without intention of paying back

_____ Keeping God's tithe

_____ Taking "souvenirs," such as towels, from hotels

_____ Not giving a day's work for a day's pay

_____ Not giving a day's pay for a day's work

_____ Operating a gambling establishment

_____ Withholding knowledge of salvation from someone who doesn't know Christ

During this exercise, did you discover weak spots in your life that should be made right with God, and perhaps with some person? If so, what will you do to make things right?

_____

NINE

GOD SAID...

You shall not give false testimony against your neighbor (Exodus 20:16).

In its simplest form, this command refers to giving false evidence in a court of law. Before justice can be done, judge and jury must know the facts. For this to happen, they must hear reliable witnesses. A false witness can defeat justice, rob another of his property, his freedom, and even his very life. A false witness is always a liar. [10]

There's an old adage: Sticks and stones may break my bones, but words can never harm me. But more accurate are the words from Shakespeare's *Othello*:

> Who robs my purse steals trash…
> But he who filches from me my good name
> Robs me of that which enriches him not
> And makes me poor indeed.

JESUS SAID...

*"By your words you will be acquitted, and by your words*_____"
(Matthew 12:37).
Jesus described Satan as *"a murderer from the beginning, not holding to the truth, for*_____
_____" (John 8:44).

In contrast, Jesus said, "I am_____
_____" (John 14:6). Therefore, no one can be indwelt by Christ and be a liar.[11]

WHAT ABOUT YOU?

Check examples of lying that you have observed. Underline any that have damaged you.
_____ False witness in court
_____ Flattery
_____ Exaggeration
_____ Half–truths
_____ Silence, in not coming to the defense of someone being slandered
_____ Slander
_____ Other_____

RESPOND

Pray. Ask God to guard and guide your tongue. Personalize Philippians 4:8. Consider ending
your prayer with Psalm 19:14: *May the words of my mouth and the meditation of my heart be
pleasing in your sight, O LORD, my Rock and my Redeemer.* Amen.

TEN

GOD SAID...

You shall not covet... (Exodus 20:17).

JESUS SAID...

*"Watch out! Be on your guard against all kinds of greed; a man's life does not consist in*_____
_____" (Luke 12:15).

REFLECTING...

My husband recalls playing with marbles as a child. At first it was just a game, but before long he began to get a feeling inside. His problem wasn't marbles; he could have bought more for pennies. The problem was *whose* marbles they were. Fortunately, his mother noticed his marble pile growing, and when she learned he was playing "for keeps," that was the end of it.

"How thankful I am," he says. "The day would have come when I outgrew marbles, of course, but by then I would have had my eyes on things much bigger!"

WHAT ABOUT YOU?

Check those that apply.

____ I covet others' coming to Christ, and I'm patient when the worship service goes into "overtime."

____ I tithe out of duty rather than from a desire of my heart.

____ I covet obedience to all of God's commands.

____ I become uncomfortable when conversation turns to Christ, preferring to talk about business or sports.

____ I covet a pure heart.

____ I covet time alone with God.

NOW WHAT?

Do you consider yourself obedient to God in all aspects of life? ____ Yes ____ No

Do you have a changed attitude toward sin?   ____ Yes ____ No

Are you able to live unattached to the world? ____ Yes ____ No

RESPOND

Petition God's help in seeking things that please Him.

Read and personalize Matthew 6:32–33: Lord Jesus, I will seek first Your kingdom and Your righteousness, believing Your promise that all these "things" will be given to me as well.

Consider ending your prayer with Psalm 119:10–11.

I seek you with all my heart; do not let me stray from your commands. I have hidden your word in my heart that I might not sin against you.

Sign your name and date it.

Signature _____ Date _____

FINDING YOUR HANDS AND FEET

Whatever your hand finds to do, do it with all your might....

— Ecclesiastes 9:10

REFLECTING...

Through the years, my husband Jack has pulled into our driveway at 6:30 sharp to keep an appointment with his supper dish. One evening he arrived uncharacteristically late.

"I saw Charlie staggering down a busy two–lane road," he said. "I feared for his safety and offered him a ride, but he said, 'You don't want me in your car, Preacher.'

"I said, 'Oh, get in, Charlie,' but he argued, 'There's something in my bag you don't want in your car.'

"'Get in, Charlie,' I insisted. I took him home and got him in bed before I left."

I suspected Jack and Charlie had been together on former occasions.

"Who's Charlie?" I asked, suspecting one of Jack's "strays" – individuals he picks up along his way to minister to, who are not members of our "fine, upstanding" congregation.

"Charlie's just one of my friends," he answered, and went to wash up.

I seemed to hear Jesus saying, *"Whatever you did for one of the least of these brothers of mine, you did for me"* (Matthew 25:40).

Then I recalled something I had clipped by an anonymous author: "Would you be chief? Then serve. Would you go up? Go down. But go as low as e'er you will, the Highest has gone lower still."

My mother would have added, "A proud person has few teachers." It takes humility to find our hands and feet in serving those whom Jesus came to seek and to save. This is true, perhaps, because flesh performs service in terms of its own advantage, while sacrificial love *"is not self–seeking"* (1 Corinthians 13:5).

JESUS' EXAMPLE

Read Mark 10:35–45. In verse 43, how did Jesus describe true greatness? *"Instead,_____*
_____."

In verse 45, how did Jesus define His ministry? *"Even_____*
_____."

Jesus' biography could be summed up in one phrase from Acts 10:38: *He went around doing good....*

Write your definition of *service.*

_____

JESUS PASSED THE TEST

Jesus began His public ministry in his hometown of Nazareth by going to the synagogue on the Sabbath, as was His custom. He stood to read a prophecy concerning Himself from Isaiah 61:1[2].

Read the incident in Luke 4:18–21. List five things Isaiah prophesied that God anointed Jesus to do.

_____

_____

_____

_____

_____

Did Jesus believe that He completed the work God had sent Him to do?

Write John 17:4. "I have_____
_____."

JESUS WANTS US TO PASS THE TEST

Hearing a dispute among His disciples concerning which of them was greatest, Jesus demonstrated true greatness by washing His disciples' feet. Then he contrasted two groups of people.

Read and complete Luke 22:25–26.

The kings of the Gentiles lord it over them; and those who exercise authority over them call themselves Benefactors. But you_____

_____.

Contrast "benefactors" of Luke 22:25–26 to "servants" of Matthew 25:31–40.

BENEFACTORS	SERVANTS
Luke 22:25–26	**Matthew 25:31–40**
Desire to lord over the helpless	Willing to_____
Moved among the rich and powerful	Moved among_____
In the judgment, will hear Jesus speak words of Matthew 25, verse 41	Will hear Jesus speak _____ _____ _____

WHO FAILS THE TEST?

Read Matthew 25:31–46.

Avoid seeing this passage as teaching salvation by good works. A trivial reading might suggest that helping one's neighbor is sufficient for earning salvation, but that isn't what the passage teaches. Nobody in history was ever saved by good works.[1] There are two groups who will hear Jesus say, "_____" (Matthew 25:41):

1. Those who refuse, or neglect, to make Jesus the Lord of their lives.
John 14:6. Jesus said, "*I am _____.*"
The writer of Hebrews 2:3 asked, "*How_____?*"

2.   Those who seek to achieve righteousness through their own efforts.

Complete Ephesians 2:8–9. *"It is by_____*
_____."

WHO PASSES THE TEST?

Jesus spoke Matthew 25 to show that the nature of the Christian life issues into good works. Paul wrote in Ephesians 2:10: *"We are_____*
_____."

So, while it's a Christian's nature to *do* good works, it isn't biblical that living a good life or performing good deeds results in salvation. We are saved only *by* God's grace *through* our faith in Christ's death on the cross.

In **Matthew 25:40** Jesus said, *"I tell you the truth,_____*
_____."

Who is included in *"these brothers of mine"*?
_____ Fellow Jews _____ Only Christians _____ Those Jesus described in Matthew 12: 50

List those whom Jesus included in *"the least of these."*
_____

What do they all have in common?
_____

THINK SMALL

Knowing where to begin is the difficult part. Our society thinks and dreams big, and plans extravagantly. In contrast, God thinks small.

▶ Jesus fed over five thousand people with five barley biscuits and two small fish from a picnic lunch offered by a small boy (John 6:1–15).
▶ Moses parted the Red Sea with his shepherd's stick, and a whole nation walked through on dry land toward the Promised Land (Exodus 14:15–16).
▶ David killed Goliath, the Philistine giant, with one small pebble targeted correctly (1 Samuel 17:50).

▶ The Woman of Samaria won a town to Jesus with one sentence: *"Come, see a man who told me everything I ever did"* (John 4:29).

▶ Andrew brought one person, Simon, to Jesus; Simon became Peter, the "Rock" of the early Church (John 1:41–42).

▶ Jesus likened the Kingdom of heaven to little children (Matthew 19:14).

THE TEST

From Matthew 25:35, personalize six acts by which you will be judged righteous. In reality you did them for Christ. For example:

_____ Someone was hungry and _____

_____ _____

_____ _____

_____ _____

_____ _____

_____ _____

Check the above deeds you're most comfortable performing.

Still thinking small, describe a time when someone reached out to you. Chances are, he or she didn't hand you something big, like money for college or down payment on a house. More likely, it was a small deed of kindness you'll never forget.

_____

_____

Describe a time when you reached out to someone.

_____

_____

Read Matthew 25:31–46 again.

Noting Matthew 25, verses 37 and 44, what will the *blessed* and *cursed* have in common?

_____

How will they differ? (v. 46).

_____

_____

THE PREREQUISITE TO SERVICE

What question did both groups ask the Lord? (vv. 37, 44). "_____?"

In your opinion, why is it characteristic of the "blessed" to be surprised that they passed the test? Why is it characteristic of the "cursed" to ask the question, "When did we see you?"

_____

We are all guilty of "not seeing." How often have we said, "The day was gone before I knew it," or "The worship service was over before I knew it," or "The children grew up before I knew it"? More accurately, "These things came and went because we did not turn aside to see them."

How many times have we stood beneath a canopy of stars and not "seen" them? How many times have we failed to value our work, the privilege of citizenship in earthly and spiritual kingdoms, the love of God, the joy of salvation, the power of prayer, and the depth of cherished friendships?

List things you will, like Moses, *turn aside to see* from now on.

_____

_____

REFLECTING...

One of my sweetest memories is of an elderly friend called "Mammy Jones." She grew flowers for patients she didn't know personally who were in a hospital near her home. She "turned aside" to *see* them and tell them about Jesus when the occasion arose because, in looking at them, she saw Christ.

I love the legend of Martin of Tours, the soldier saint. On a winter day he entered a city and met a beggar asking alms. Martin had nothing to give, but the beggar shivered with cold, so Martin took off his cloak and placed it around the beggar, who blessed Martin and disappeared. That night, Martin dreamed that he stood before Jesus at the Judgment Seat of Christ. Jesus was seated on His throne with the hosts of heaven surrounding Him, wearing that cloak! [2]

Little is much in Jesus' hand. It isn't our ability, but our *availability*, that God wants. He places high value on the smallest deed born out of love for "one of the least of these," the wounded of the world. Suffering is universal and all around us. It stands behind us in a check–out line, lives in houses next door, and sits beside us in church.

Comparing Matthew 25:34–40 with the daily performance of your hands and feet, what actions, if any, will you take to bring your attitude and deeds into line with those of Christ who *"went about doing good"*?

_____

_____

_____

A NEW TESTAMENT EXAMPLE

Read Luke 10:25–37.

The parable of the Good Samaritan has nudged the conscience of the world for centuries, and has served as the supreme model of finding one's hands and feet. Jesus told the story after being asked by an expert in the law, *"Who is my neighbor?"*

Jesus, answering, began, *"A man was*_____

_____*."*

The robbers' attack included what acts of violence?

_____

With Jerusalem 2,300 feet above sea level and Jericho 1,300 feet below sea level, in little more than twenty miles, the road between the two cities dropped 3,600 feet,[3] winding through mountainous country where limestone caves offered ambush for robbers.

No doubt, many of those traveling with Jesus had walked along the road known as the "Bloody Pass," and could picture sudden turns in the road where travelers were subject to unforeseen dangers.

The priest in the story was a Jew, and was, by divine calling, any Jew's "neighbor." No doubt, at times he had preached on the virtues of helping the needy. The Levite was an usher in the temple and a member of the order from which singers were chosen for the Levite choir. Jesus made it clear that both priest and Levite *saw* the wounded man, but passed by on the other side of the road.[4]

But a Samaritan, as he traveled, came where the man was (v. 33).

Samaritans were half–breeds, belonging to a race that Jews held in religious disdain because, as citizens of the Northern Kingdom, exiled to Assyria, they had intermarried with their Assyrian conquerors during exile.[5]

Write phrases that prove the Samaritan dismissed fears about robbers.

He_____.

He_____.

He_____.

Who, in your opinion, *was* this man who had been left for dead?

_____ Someone the Samaritan recognized _____ His business partner

_____ An unknown person in need

In pain, the wounded man watched two men in clerical dress approaching, who would surely help. Why do you think they *passed by on the other side*?

_____ They didn't know him.

_____ They would have been "unclean" if they touched blood.

_____ They were on their way to a meeting for "Making the Road from Jerusalem to Jericho Safer."

_____ The man didn't fit their description of a "neighbor."

WHAT ABOUT YOU?

At first glance, it's easy to judge these two, but can you be certain you would have behaved differently?

Approaching the wounded man, what might you have thought?

_____ "Thank God it didn't happen to me!"

_____ "I'll do what I can."

_____ "He should have known not to travel this road alone."

_____ "I have no first–aid equipment with me."

_____ Other_____

Who are the "wounded" you know?

_____ Someone widowed or permanently injured

_____ A neighbor laid off or fired from their job

_____ An invalid

_____ A victim of abuse

_____ Someone undergoing separation or divorce

_____ Victim of natural disaster

_____ Other_____

YOU CAN GET THERE FROM HERE

In using your hands and feet, begin where you are with what you have. Your rewards will be based on simple acts of kindness in the Judgment. Contrast the "Blessed" to the "Cursed" of Matthew 25:34–40.

BLESSED	CURSED
Their help is uncalculating. They never think of piling up eternal merits, but help because they cannot keep from helping.	If they could know it is Jesus they are helping, _____ _____
They ask no reward, nor count cost.	When helping promises praise or any publicity, they help, but that is disguised selfishness, not help.[6]
They change plans, use their own resources, and interrupt schedules to put love into action.	They form committees, _____ _____ _____

MOSES' HANDS AND FEET

Read Exodus 1–4.

When God called Moses to lead the Israelites out of Egyptian slavery, Moses was eighty years old. A Hebrew by birth, he was reared as an Egyptian prince in the palace of the pharaoh. Moses had been divinely prepared and positioned for the job. He spoke both languages, understood both cultures, and commanded respect from both worlds.

At the time of his "call," Moses was hiding in the Midian desert to escape Pharaoh's wrath after killing an Egyptian who had been mistreating a Hebrew. Exodus 3:2 records that as Moses tended the sheep of Jethro, his father–in–law, *the angel of the LORD*_____

Fire symbolized God's presence. As Moses approached to investigate the burning bush, God called his name. Moses answered, *"Here I am."* God instructed Moses to remove his shoes, then He identified Himself. He told Moses He had heard the cries of His people in Egypt and, being concerned for their suffering, was sending Moses to bring the Israelites out of Egypt.

No doubt Moses was elated to hear that God was going to free the Hebrews from their slavery. It was when God appointed *him* to deliver them that Moses resisted.

Paraphrase Moses' excuses for not accepting God's offer.
EXAMPLE:

SCRIPTURE	MOSES' EXCUSE	GOD'S ANSWER
1. Exodus 3:11–12	**"Who am I to do this?"**	**"I will be with you."**
2. Exodus 3:13–14	_____	_____
3. Exodus 4:1–4	_____	_____
4. Exodus 4:10–12	_____	_____
5. Exodus 4:13–15	_____	I will send _____
		_____
		_____

"SIGNS" FROM GOD

1. Exodus 4:2–5. Moses' shepherd's staff became_____."
2. Exodus 4:6–7. Moses' hand_____.
3. Exodus 4:8–9. Should Pharaoh not believe him, Moses was to pour_____

_____

TRUE / FALSE

____ God still calls people to work for Him.

____ God knows our names and our locations.

____ Needing "signs" is evidence of a weak faith.

____ God begins where we are and uses what we have.

____ God takes meager resources and turns them into major assets.

____ Difficulties in answering God's call are real.

____ God can become angry when we offer excuses for not following His will.

REFLECTING...

I experienced God's call one day at 4:15 a.m. I woke startled by the realization that I should write a letter to a man I barely knew. God's call was clear: I was to explain salvation, how he could become a Christian, and the urgency of his doing so.

My excuses echoed Moses': "Ask Jack; he's the pastor."
Silence.

"I hardly know the man; he could get the wrong impression."
Silence.

"What will I say to this almost–stranger?"

"I will write the letter."

I shot out of bed and took the stairs two at a time to Jack's study. Never have I written eight pages so fast, nor am I capable of writing anything so well. Later that morning, I mailed it with a prayer.

Sunday came. From my place in the choir I watched the man enter the church and awkwardly locate a seat. Before long, he joined the church and was baptized.

I call that experience my "burning bush," and will walk by the light of its fire the rest of my days.

WHAT ABOUT YOU?

Have you experienced a "burning bush" when God called you to a specific task? Explain.

_____

_____

How did you answer? _____ Here am I, Lord. _____ Someone else can do a better job.
_____ I'm too busy/tired/sleepy. _____ I'm not qualified. _____ I'm off to the lake/mountains.
_____ Other_____

Don't wait with Moses to see a bush on fire. Most of God's calls are heard out of our deep concern for the physical and spiritual needs of the world about us.

There is a "bush" that burns in all of us. Even now God is asking, *"What is that in your hand?"*

Study your hands. They're wonderfully designed to do God's will. Meditate on ways Jesus' hands blessed others. List different ministries Jesus performed with His hands. Check John 21:9–14; Mark 7:32; Mark 9:27; Mark 10:13.

_____

_____

_____

Look at your feet. In Matthew 28:19–20, Jesus called His followers to *"make disciples of all nations"* at a time when transportation was mainly by foot. He hasn't canceled His "Great Commission."

How can you share Christ with someone nearby?

_____

_____

With someone far away? (Malachi 3:10)

_____

With your tithe? (Luke 11:42)

_____

How do you think the Pharisees responded?

_____

What's *your* response?

_____

NOW WHAT?

In the Judgment, we want Jesus' commendation. Write Matthew 25:21."*Well done,*_____

_____."

What is in your hand?
____ A can of soup for my sick neighbor
____ A tool I can lend

_____ Jumper cables

_____ Food for the homeless

_____ Salvation tracts

_____ Thank–you notes to people who shared Christ with me

_____ Clothes for charity

_____ Time for visiting residents in a health center

_____ A telephone to invite someone to church

_____ Other_____

Write your plans for reaching out in Jesus' name to someone in need.

_____

_____

SPIRITUAL CHECK-UP

Generations ago, it was proper to sign correspondence, "Your obedient servant." We don't do that today. Imagining ourselves as servants is foreign to us, yet Paul insisted in Philippians 2:5–16, that we follow Jesus' example.

Verse 7. How did Jesus respond to His equality with God?

_____

_____

Verse 8. What act of supreme humility did Jesus perform?

_____

_____

Verse 9. What resulted from His obedience?

_____

_____

Reading the passage, I feel Paul taking my spiritual temperature, and probing my attitude toward life, and people, including those fallen by the waysides of life – the "Charlies" who delay my suppertime.

Jesus surrounded himself with the "Charlies" of His world. He never got used to sin, sickness, poverty, and loneliness. Neither must we. No doubt many we stoop to serve won't be clean, likeable, or appreciative, but we follow Christ and have our orders. The day will come when everyone – believers, atheists, agnostics, and those who waver between two opinions *will bow* ... *and every*_____

_____(Philippians 2:10–11).

God offers two choices: Bow before Jesus as Savior and Lord in this life, or bow before Him later as Judge (Matthew 25:41–46). Thankfully, you chose the former time for bowing, both by receiving Him as Savior, and by serving others for whom He died. And, while you were not saved by works (Ephesians 2:8–9), you were saved *by* God's grace *through* faith that *will* work (verse 10).

RESPONDING...

Often during my quiet time, I read Scripture, write my response, and sign it. It's like writing a "thank–you" note to Jesus for performing a miracle in my life.

Please share my recent note to Him:

> Lord, You worked *for* me on the cross. Thank You!
> You worked *in* me when I was born again. Thank You!
> Now You seek to work *through* me – through my witness, influence, and ministry. In my imperfect love I'll serve others, knowing that whatever I do for one of the least of these, I do it unto You. Thank You, Lord, that by Your example, you have shown me ... *my hands and feet.*"

Your obedient servant, _____ Date_____

LEARNING TO SHARE

I am not ashamed of the gospel, because it is the power of God for the salvation of everyone who believes....

— Romans 1:16

REFLECTING...

I remember the first time I shared my faith. Along with my husband Jack and our daughters, I attended a witnessing training session at Lake Junaluska, North Carolina. The first evening session featured a moving message by the seminar leader. The following morning, while situating our little girls in their age–appropriate seminars, I missed the important training session.

The afternoon arrived with my expecting another message. I settled into my chair for the session. only to learn that we were going out in pairs to share our faith. We would be driven to assigned streets at two o'clock and be picked up at five o'clock. No spouses could go together. My heart sank as I watched Jack walk away to join his partner.

Just then the speaker requested those without partners to assemble down front to be paired. My spirit trembled as every person in the auditorium rose to fulfill the Great Commission of Matthew 28:19–20… except me. I reluctantly rose and walked to the front. A young woman approached, asking, "Will you be my partner?" She later told me that while I said, "Yes," I shook my head "No."

"Nan, will you go first?" I begged, hoping to watch a presentation before giving one.

"Yes, but every other house is yours," she said.

No one answered at the first house.

"The next house is yours," she reminded me.

Feeling sick and trembling, I rang the doorbell.

Please, Lord, don't let anyone be at home.

A smiling lady opened the door.

I explained that we were in the neighborhood sharing our faith. Might we come in?

Lord, please don't let her invite us in!

"Follow me to the den," she said, "it's cooler there."

Lord, if You make me do this, I'll cry!

I kept my promise. Holding the little booklet, my hands and voice trembled throughout the presentation, and I began to cry when I asked if she would commit her life to Christ.

She eagerly said yes.

"I will," she said, "<u>because you have wept over my sins</u>. Even I have never wept over my sins. And may I have that little book? My son will come home at four o'clock, and he's not a Christian either."

I watched God bring two people into the Kingdom that afternoon; it changed my life forever. Back at the conference center, I rushed to tell Jack, "God opened doors and hearts, but when He opened my mouth, I cried."

"Didn't I tell you?" he asked. "Your greatest ability is your *availability*. God uses what you offer Him. If you offer laughter, He uses laughter; if you give Him tears, He uses tears."

Read Matthew 28: 16–20.
Picture Jesus on a mountain following His resurrection. Place yourself in the crowd that some Bible scholars believe comprised the *"more than 500…"* described in 1 Corinthians 15:6.

The fact that *"some doubted"* bears this out, suggesting that more than the eleven apostles were present, since they were, by then, confirmed believers. Our Lord's ascension did not take place at this time, but later, after He ministered to His disciples in Jerusalem (Luke 24:44–53).[1]

Write Matthew 28:19–20, Jesus' "Great Commission."

_____

_____

_____

RESEARCH

The verb _go_ in this passage is more accurately translated as the present participle _going._ Jesus said, _"Therefore, while going in the world, make disciples."_ Regardless, then, of where we go, we are to share our faith in Him.[2]

Jesus' plan for winning the world is singular; we are to share our spiritual possessions with secular people. He has no alternate plan. Once we accept His plan in Matthew 28:19–20 as our own, and shape our lives and ministries around it, our prayer becomes, "Father, is my present activity in step with Your plan for winning the world to Christ?"

In order for our plan to be His plan:

▶ **We must verbally declare our faith.**
Living a good life isn't enough to win others to Christ. (See Acts 11:20 and Matthew 28:10.) No one ever says, "I've observed your life, therefore Jesus died for my sins." Why? Because a life can't talk, only lips can speak.

▶ **Our lives must, however, verify our speech.**
Ron Hutchcraft wrote, "Most people do not come to believe in Jesus without first believing in a follower of Jesus. When our Lord said, _"In the same way, let your light shine before men, that they may see your good deeds and praise your Father in heaven"_ (Matthew 5:16), Jesus meant that showing others by the way we live is what would interest them in the relationship that makes us tick. But we must show and tell! Yes, their salvation depends entirely upon their choice to accept or reject Christ, but their decision to live eternally with God or to die without hope, may hinge upon our obedience to "go and tell" (Matthew 28:10). [3]

Jesus came to earth on a rescue mission, and calls us as believers to join Him. Whenever rescue is needed, when it comes to eternal life or death, _proximity_ equals _responsibility._ Where you and I are on the scene, we are responsible – not for their _decision,_ but for our obedience in sharing the good news of salvation. [4]

SPIRITUAL CHECK-UP

Are you a "rescuer"? Mark your choices.

At the beach, I see	____ vacationers	____ lost people
At ball games, I see	____ fans	____ lost people
At malls, I see	____ shoppers	____ lost people
At my work, I see	____ co–workers	____ lost people
At school, I see	____ students	____ lost people

Jesus was a rescuer. How did He see large groups of people?

Write Mark 6:34.

_____

_____

RESEARCH

The Greek word the apostle Mark used for "compassion" is *splagchnisthesis*. It is the strongest word in the Greek language for compassionate pity. It's a compassion that moves a person to the depths of his being. The term is used only of Jesus in the New Testament.[5]

Match Scriptures with conditions that aroused Jesus' compassion:

SCRIPTURE	CONDITION THAT AROUSED JESUS' COMPASSION
Example:	
Matthew 9:36	**harassment and dejection**
Matthew 14:14	_____
Matthew 15:32	_____
Matthew 20:34	_____
Mark 1:41	_____
Mark 6:34	_____
Luke 7:13	_____

SPIRITUAL CHECK-UP

Read Psalm 139.

Before you accepted Christ, what conditions in your life might have moved Jesus to compassion?

_____

_____

List present conditions.

_____

_____

List verses in the psalm you relate most to today.

_____

_____

REMEMBER...

Fear is normal.

When I first began sharing my faith, I feared the unknown factors in witnessing. How would I be received? Would I offend the person and "bruise the fruit"?

I soon discovered that God was already at work in the lives of the people He sent me to, whether to plant, cultivate, or harvest a soul. It was always easier than I anticipated because God's Spirit inspired my words.

Consider this: Sharing your faith so that others have the opportunity to live eternally with Christ is the most righteous, unselfish thing you can ever do. Picture them at the judgment seat of Christ hearing Christ tell them ***"Come, you who are blessed by my Father; take your inheritance, the kingdom prepared for you since the creation of the world." Then picture Him telling you, "Well done!"***

Lack of knowledge is okay.

Do you believe your listener will ask questions you can't answer? Can you memorize a few Bible verses? You already know John 3:16. There are also great tracts available to read together with your listener.

I like sharing the booklet, *"Have You Heard of the Four Spiritual Laws?"* [6] As I read it aloud to my listeners, they hear God speaking His Words, not Catherine speaking hers.

In addition, I have memorized enough Scripture to develop what Ron Hutchcraft calls "My Testimony Tool Kit" which I use to craft testimonies to fit the situation at hand. Jesus used this method exclusively. (See John 3 and 4.) Paul was also a master at it. (See 1 Corinthians 9:20–22.) I can talk about how Jesus makes a difference in my life during loneliness, depression, being a marriage partner, parenting, or stress. It's easy to draw people into conversation about Christ when they mention such topics. [7]

REFLECTING...

Using my tool kit, I engaged a lawyer in conversation in a small café in Halifax, Nova Scotia. Bragging about his successful court case, he strode from table to table getting to know people. I drew him into conversation that led to the Cross by asking if he were prepared for his eternal court case. He said flippantly, "In the judgment I will do what Job did – put my fist in God's face and plead my case!"

"But, sir, the verdict is already in. The only verdict in God's courtroom is "Guilty as charged," and the sentence is eternal separation from God. Paul said, *"all have sinned and fall short of the glory of God"* (Romans 3:23), and *"the wages of sin is death, but the gift of God is eternal life in Christ Jesus our Lord"* (Romans 6:23).

"Someone is carrying your sins right now," I said. "If you are carrying them, you'll pay for them with eternal death. If Jesus is carrying them, your sins are already paid for by His sacrificial death on the cross. If you should die tonight, will you wake up in heaven with God?"

"I honestly don't know," he answered. His eyes were set on me, as if considering the matter for the first time.

"Where do you want to wake up?" I asked.

"Lady," he barely whispered, "I want to be where you are."

"You can be," I said. "May I sit here and explain how to be in heaven with God?"

God won the case with a "Courtroom" testimony from my tool kit.

God uses my "Pain Testimony" whenever I relate how God healed me from rheumatoid arthritis. Then I discuss the even greater "sin disease" we all need healing from and explain the Cross.

I use my "Contract Testimony" when signing a contract, saying, "Before you go, could we discuss an *eternal* contract?" I explain that everyone has signed a contract either with God or the enemy. Directing the discussion toward the Cross, I invite the person to receive Christ as Savior. Using my tool kit is a natural way to guide conversations toward Jesus.

You don't have to be an "expert witness."

Simply state what Jesus has done in your life. Many effective testimonies in Scripture are one–liners. The woman of Samaria led a whole town to Christ with her famous statement, recorded in John 4:29: "_____."

In John 1:36, John the Baptist said, "_____."

My favorite "one–liner" was spoken by the man who was born blind. Pressured by the Pharisees to identify Jesus as the person who healed him on the Sabbath, and to describe the manner in which he was healed, the man answered "_____
_____" (John 9:25).

I use the man's answer whenever I'm asked "smoke–screen" questions, such as, "Where did Cain get his wife?" or "Did Adam have a belly button?" I answer, "I don't know the answer to that, but one thing I *do* know: Once I was 'blind,' and now I see!" That answer draws my listener back to Christ.

THE STORY ONLY YOU CAN TELL

Your personal testimony is your most powerful tool in witnessing because no one can dispute it. Your experience was powerful enough to bring you to faith in Christ. It will encourage others to profess faith in Him also.

Read Acts 26:2–23.

Paul provided the perfect outline in Acts 26. His conversion was so life–changing that he was compelled to share it. He shaped his story the following way:

> 1. A gracious introduction, including a compliment for his listener (Acts 26:2–3)
> 2. A description of his life before he met Christ (verses 4–11)
> 3. His realization that God was seeking him (verse 15)

4. His turning point from sin and self to Christ (verse 13)

5. A description of his life after becoming a Christian (verse 19)

Let's write our stories using Paul's outline.

A GRACIOUS INTRODUCTION

PAUL'S INTRODUCTION

Acts 26:2–3. *"King Agrippa, I consider myself fortunate to stand before you today as I make my defense against all the accusations of the Jews, and especially so because you are well acquainted with all the Jewish customs and controversies."*

Notice that Paul paid Agrippa two compliments. Underline them.

MY INTRODUCTION

It's always an honor to share my Christian experience with those who are interested in knowing more about Christ as I believe you are.

YOUR INTRODUCTION

_____

_____

_____

_____

_____

LIFE BEFORE KNOWING CHRIST

PAUL'S STORY

A.   The good part, Acts 26:4–8.

"The Jews all know the way I have lived ever since I was a child ... that according to the strictest sect of our religion, I lived as a Pharisee...."

B. The bad part, verses 9–11.

"I too was convinced that I ought to do all that was possible to oppose the name of Jesus of Nazareth…. On the authority of the chief priests I put many of the saints in prison, and when they were put to death, I cast my vote against them….

"I went from one synagogue to another to have them punished, and I tried to force them to blaspheme…. I even went to foreign cities to persecute them."

MY STORY

A. The good part

Growing up, I owned few luxuries. Requesting something new was often countered with instructions on how to manage without it. Hopscotch, jump rope, and "kick the can" were favorite games. For entertainment I wrote poetry and played the out–of–tune piano by the dim light from a single bulb hanging by a drop cord from the ceiling in our unheated living room.

Reading was my favorite hobby; in fact, I read so many books that the bookmobile stopped at our house. As for religion, I cut my spiritual teeth on the *Proverbs* and the *Ten Commandments* and wise sayings Mama quoted. I am eternally grateful to my parents for teaching me to live a godly life.

B. The bad part

Even though I read voraciously, I never read the Bible. My biblical knowledge was rooted in Old Testament teachings more than in the gospels. I was aware that Christmas marked Jesus' birth, and Easter celebrated His resurrection, but I saw no connection between those events and my personal life or my eternal destination. Neither did I understand that Jesus died on the cross to pay the penalty for my sins, and rose from the dead in order to live in my heart through the power of the Holy Spirit. In fact, I was unaware that I was a sinner at all, and rarely thought about the world to come.

YOUR STORY

A. The good part

_____

_____

_____

_____

_____
_____
_____
_____

B. The bad part

_____
_____
_____
_____
_____
_____

PAUL'S "WAKE-UP CALL"

Acts 26:12–14. *"On one of these journeys I was going to Damascus with the authority and commission of the chief priests. About noon, O king, as I was on the road, I saw a light from heaven, brighter than the sun, blazing around me and my companions. We all fell to the ground, and I heard a voice saying to me in Aramaic, 'Saul, Saul, why do you persecute me? It is hard for you to kick against the goads.'"*

MY "WAKE-UP CALL"

Each spring our community church held a week of revival services. At the end of every sermon, the preacher invited people to "come forward and receive Christ." At twelve years of age I realized that the preacher's invitation included me. His sermon had declared me a sinner separated from God and the result he described did not sound favorable. I experienced a mysterious desire to respond, but not understanding my rights as a potential child of God, and not knowing the questions to ask, I virtually stood at the cross, my heart and mind open and receptive, waiting for a future encounter with God.

YOUR "WAKE-UP CALL"

_____
_____
_____

_____

_____

_____

_____

PAUL'S TURNING POINT

Acts 26:15–18. *"Then I asked, 'Who are you, Lord?' 'I am Jesus, whom you are persecuting,' the Lord replied. 'Now get up and stand on your feet. I have appeared to you to appoint you as a servant and as a witness of what you have seen of me and what I will show you. I will rescue you from your own people and from the Gentiles. I am sending you to them to open their eyes and turn them from darkness to light, and from the power of Satan to God, so that they may receive forgiveness of sins and a place among those who are sanctified by faith in me.'"*

MY TURNING POINT

One night, years later, my college dorm counselor asked me to take a message to a girl who roomed upstairs. Approaching her room, I saw the door ajar and heard a voice. Assuming that girls were chatting, I pushed open her door. I was shocked to see a girl on her knees, talking out loud to God!

Feeling like an intruder, I backed into the hall, froze, and waited for silence. Then I knocked, relayed the message, and returned to my room. But I returned a different person, knowing that I had not just opened the door to her room; I had opened the door to the throne room of God.

The next morning, the desire I'd had as a child to answer the preacher's invitation returned. Through the years and across the miles I heard him pleading, "Come home to Christ who died for you!"

But there was no aisle to walk down, and no minister waiting to take my hand – only the memory of a girl praying out loud on her knees. I said, "Lord, I don't know what or *how* to ask, *but* whatever You did in that girl's life, will You do in my life now?"

Had you been present, you might have said, "I didn't see anything happen."

Neither did I. There was no blinding light from heaven, no ringing bells, no angels playing harps. Only one thing: There was Jesus keeping His promise in Revelation 3:20: *"Here I am! I stand at the door and knock. If anyone hears my voice and opens the door, I will come in...."*

YOUR TURNING POINT

PAUL'S LIFE AFTER TRUSTING CHRIST

Acts 26:19–20. *"So then, King Agrippa, I was not disobedient to the vision from heaven. First to those in Damascus, then to those in Jerusalem and in all Judea, and to the Gentiles also, I preached that they should repent and turn to God and prove their repentance by their deeds."*

MY LIFE SINCE TRUSTING CHRIST

Paul said in 2 Corinthians 5:17, *"Therefore, if anyone is in Christ, he is a new creation; the old has gone, the new has come!"*

How am I new? Many things that once were important to me have become minor. Things I once considered unimportant are now top priority. I laugh where once I wept; I weep where once I laughed. Except for Jesus, I would have married differently, reared children differently, lived another lifestyle, chosen a different career, and traveled a far different road to my eternal destination.

While I would like to say that I've been perfect since the day I received Christ, I confess that I'm not in shouting distance of perfection. I've learned, however, the meaning of Colossians 2:6–7: *So then, just as you received Christ Jesus as Lord, continue to live in him, rooted and built up in him, strengthened in the faith … and overflowing with thankfulness.*

Am I making sense? Have you experienced anything like this?

YOUR LIFE SINCE TRUSTING CHRIST

NOTE: If Christ was always the center of your home, as He was in young Timothy's (2 Timothy 1:5), you may not know the moment of your conversion. Stress what it was like to grow up in a Christian home, how you made your faith public, and how your life has been different because of Christ. You might include: "If it hadn't been for Christ, I...."

_____

_____

_____

_____

_____

_____

_____

CHECKLIST

Be sure you:

1. Include the gospel in a nutshell: Christ died for your sins, was buried, rose again, and now lives in you through the presence of the Holy Spirit.
2. Make it clear that becoming a Christian hasn't made you perfect, and that you continually need and seek forgiveness.
3. Balance the length of your subtitles as much as possible. Don't *announce* subtitles; they're for your use only.
4. Eliminate proper names of places and people that divert people's thinking.
5. Keep your story conversational.
6. Use no more than two or three Scriptures so you won't sound "preachy."

MY RESPONSE

"Father, thank you for rescuing me from sin through the death of Your Son Jesus. In response, I want to rescue others and help change the world. Teach me to see the people who don't know You the way Jesus saw them – harassed and helpless – and feel compassion for them. Make me like the Christian Paul described in 2 Corinthians 3:3: *You show that you are a letter from Christ … written not with ink but with the Spirit of the living God, not on tablets of stone but on tablets of human hearts.*

"Lord, multiply my life with other believers. Open doors of opportunity for sharing my faith, open hearts to be receptive to Your Word, and open my mouth to speak Your praise…*with laughter … or with tears.*" Amen.

YOUR RESPONSE

_____

_____

_____

_____

_____

_____

_____

_____

Signature _____ Date _____

LESSON 12

LEARNING TO WALK

Show me the way I should go, for to you I lift up my soul.

— Psalm 143:8

REFLECTING...

There's an old adage that goes: "The longest journey begins with a single step."

I remember our daughter Tamara's first steps. Jack and I delayed her walking, believing it would be easier for my sister to keep her in a walker while he and I attended a convention. Returning home, Jack carried her to the soft grass in our back yard. He stood her alone, hurried away, and motioned her to come to him. She laughed and ran into his arms!

While I can't remember my first physical steps, I took my first spiritual ones at age nineteen. Most Christians accept Christ much younger than nineteen, thus my spiritual steps, like Tamara's physical ones, were delayed until seeing a girl on her knees in prayer beckoned me to Christ. Once invited, I ran joyfully into God's arms.

Because the Jews had anticipated their Messiah for centuries, one would expect that when He stepped from eternity onto the earth He had created, they would have run to Him in joyful acceptance. John, however, records three different responses to Him.

Read John 1:10–13 and match the following:

	GROUP	RESPONSE
Verse 10:	*the world*	*became children of God*
Verse 11:	*his own*	*did not receive him*
Verse 12:	*those who believed in his name*	*did not recognize him*

THE DISCIPLES' FIRST STEPS

Read John 1:35–51.

Assuming the unnamed disciple in verse 35 was John, name the first four disciples to walk with Jesus.

_____

John 1:43: With what words did Jesus beckon Philip to walk with Him?

_____

John 1:46: Who hesitated and questioned before following Jesus?

_____

Matthew 9:9: Who left a lucrative business to walk with Him?

_____

WHAT ABOUT YOU?

What does walking with God mean to you? Choose <u>one</u> response.
_____ Wanting the eternal life that Jesus provides
_____ Committing my mind, will, and emotions to His lordship
_____ Experiencing that which excites my mind and stirs my emotions

Why are the other responses inadequate?

_____

Check the most accurate description of your first spiritual steps.
_____ Like Andrew and John, I followed Jesus the moment I met Him.
_____ Like Nathanael, I settled all my doubts first.
_____ Like Matthew, I left a lifestyle or occupation to follow Christ.
_____ Other _____

You didn't reach the apex of faith the moment you were born spiritually, any more than you walked long distances immediately following your physical birth. As you mature in Christ, the gap closes between where you are and where Jesus wants you to be in your walk with Him.

The word "walk" is frequently used in Scripture to indicate faithfulness to God and fellowship with God. There is no instruction manual in the Bible for walking in the Spirit, perhaps because each Christian's walk is individual and unique. However, God asks certain things of us if we are to walk with Him.[1]

In your words, summarize Paul's advice in Ephesians 5:1–21.

Verse 1_____

Verse 2_____

Verse 3_____

Verse 4_____

Verse 6_____

Verses 7–9, 11 _____

Verses 10, 15–16 _____

Verse 17_____

_____

LEARNING TO WALK

Verse 18. Learning to walk with God is a milestone on the road to spiritual maturity. Its step–by–step motion requires active involvement. The source of our strength for walking with God is the Holy Spirit. We are controlled by Him much like a ship's movement is controlled by the wind filling its sails. While every Christian is *indwelt* by the Spirit at the moment of conversion, not every Christian is *filled,* or controlled, by the Spirit. When we are controlled by the Spirit, our minds, wills, and emotions are under His control. (Read John 14:15–21.) Our relationships with others deepen (Ephesians 5:19), our relationship to Christ becomes more joyful (v. 19), and a spirit of gratitude pervades our lives (v. 20).[2]

SPIRITUAL CHECK-UP

▶ My present walk with God is:

____ more like a crawl

____ in spurts

____ like running a race with my eye on the goal of reaching heaven

____ Other_____

▶ My walk with God began:

____ when I was a child

____ after falling into deep sin and repenting

____ when feeling empty due to walking my own way

____ following a tragedy that revealed life's fragility

____ while reading the Bible and realizing I had caved in from spiritual malnutrition

____ Other_____

▶ I walk with God:

____ when everyone else does

____ when no one is watching

____ all day, every day

Choose *one* of your responses and expound upon your thoughts about walking with God.

_____

_____

_____

BIBLICAL CHARACTERS WHO WALKED WITH GOD

Read Genesis 5:22–24, Hebrews 11:5–6, and Jude 14–16.

Genesis 5:24: "_____."

From Jude 14–16, describe world conditions when Enoch walked with God. Underline those you find prevalent in our world today.

_____

_____

Since Enoch walked with God under those conditions, can we walk with God in our generation?

_____

REWARDS FOR WALKING WITH GOD

According to Psalm 16:11, what rewards for walking with God do we receive in this life?

_____

What reward awaits us in eternity?

_____

From Hebrews 11:5, what was Enoch's unusual reward for walking with God?

_____

Why?

_____

The most noticeable thing about Enoch's life was that he walked with God. Can people say that about you? ____ Yes ____ No ____ Not yet

Explain your answer.

_____

_____

OTHERS WHO WALKED WITH GOD

Write the following Scriptures and underline individuals or groups who walked with God.

Genesis 6:9 _____

_____

Genesis 17:1_____

_____

What characteristic, included in both passages, does God expect from those who walk with Him?

_____

▶ **Leviticus 26:12**_____

To whom was God speaking? _____

▶ **Matthew 4:19**_____

Who was Jesus addressing? _____

▶ **Matthew 10:6–7** Jesus said,_____

Who are His *sheep*?_____

WHAT ABOUT YOU?

How closely do you follow Jesus?

___ At a distance, occasionally losing my way.

___ Close, because accepting guidance is better than crying for help.

Write Psalm 68:19. Underline the time when God wants us to walk with Him.

_____

CHOOSING THE NARROW ROAD

REFLECTING...

During college I performed in _Alice in Wonderland._ I especially enjoyed the scene between Alice and the Cheshire Cat:

When Alice inquired which way she should go, the cat replied, "That depends on where you _want_ to go."

"I don't _care_ where...."

"Then it doesn't matter which way you go."

"So long as I get **somewhere.**"

"Oh, you're sure to do that, if you only walk long enough." [3]

The cat was right; we're all going somewhere, and we're sure to arrive at one destination or another. Daily we travel closer to our eternal destination. Arriving safely doesn't mean that we will all enter heaven having the same degree of Christian maturity, however.

In Matthew 7:13–14, Jesus said, "_Enter_____
_____."

From the top of the Empire State Building in New York one can look down on masses of people moving in all directions. According to Jesus, they're traveling only two roads.

▶ **To which two roads did Jesus refer?**_____
In your opinion, why is the "broad" road _broad_?
_____ It's crowded. Everyone since Adam began life on it. (Psalm 51:5). "_____
_____."

_____ People insist on dragging excess "baggage" with them, requiring extra room.

List unneeded "baggage" _____

____ Leaving the crowd requires effort; most people prefer to remain where they are.

▶ **Name the only two groups walking:**_____

As a teenager, I sometimes begged for permission to go places my parents forbade, claiming "everyone else will be there." They answered, "That might be a good reason for your not going," and quoted the old adage: "You are who you run with."

▶ **Name the two destinations:**_____

By *life,* Jesus referred to life here and now, not eternal life in heaven or hell. Of course, because death has no transforming power, the road chosen in this life leads to the other side of death. Our choices shape our future. Paul, in Galatians 6:7, warned: "*A man*_____

_____." Decisions we make today will pass judgment on us when we cross the finish line of the race called *life.*

▶ **What two gates are available?**

We entered physical life through a small gate (struggling through the narrow birth canal) and began growing, but our struggles didn't stop there; they continued. Throughout life we must eat properly, get sufficient rest, fight disease, study hard, drive by rules, pursue careers, control spending, rear children by God's standards, and keep marriage healthy.

Walking the narrow road can be lonely, too, but it leads to *life*! Someone once said, "If you find yourself in a place where you have nothing left but God, you have all you need."

We sense finality in Jesus' voice as He spoke in Matthew 7:13–14 about walking with God. While many people think that it doesn't matter what a person believes so long as that person is sincere, and they argue that all religions lead to the same place anyway, there's been no word from God on that! From Jesus' standpoint, life is a journey and everyone is a traveler. We're headed somewhere, and in time we will arrive at one of two destinations.

There is no third road, gate, or destination. Jesus said, "*I am the way and the truth and the life. No one comes to the Father except through **me**"* (John 14:6).

WHAT ABOUT YOU?

Describe a time when you struggled to leave the broad road in some aspect of life. Be sure to include your rewards for having chosen the narrow road. Share your story. Consider including

God's promise in Isaiah 43:2: *When you* _____

_____

Identify "waters" you encountered, and "rivers" you crossed to enter what Jesus called *life*.

_____

_____

_____

WHEN WE TAKE THE WRONG ROAD

Many saints of God wandered from the narrow road, preferring the broad road for a season. King David's sin with Bathsheba (2 Samuel 11) and Samson's trysts with Delilah (Judges 16) are examples.

Perhaps the most famous of wrong roads appeared on the spiritual map when Adam and Eve challenged God's control of their lives. By doing so, they caused their sin to infect the entire human race. (See Genesis 2.)

As Eve approached her spiritual crossroad, she knew that the way to life through obedience lay straight ahead. When tempted, she repeated God's command forbidding her to eat from the tree in the middle of the garden (Genesis 3:2–3). Yes, she knew! But Satan attacked her physical senses and she surrendered on all counts.

Write phrases from Genesis 3:1–7 that describe Satan's attack on Eve's senses: sound, sight, smell, taste, touch.

Example:

*Sound: **She heard and embraced Satan's ideas (Genesis 3:1–7).***

Sight: _____

Smell: _____

Touch: _____

Taste: _____

Reading the remainder of Genesis 3, find and list the results of Eve's sin.

_____

_____

_____

Why do you think God created man with free will when He might have forced him to obey Him in all things?

_____

Two forces struggle for mastery over us. Write <u>Spirit</u> or <u>Flesh</u> by the following ways to recognize these forces.

_____walks by faith   _____ chooses instant, rather than delayed, gratification

_____ walks by sight   _____ chooses the spiritual over the material

_____ requires self–sacrifice _____ refers to fallen nature

_____ lives for self–gratification

Answers L-R: S, F, F, S, S, F, F

GETTING BACK ON THE NARROW ROAD

When we fall into sin, there is a way back if we choose to take it. God, not man, achieved the way. We were unable to justify ourselves, but God could and did through the death and resurrection of our Lord. God's great love is expressed in **John 3:16**:

*God*_____

_____.

We return to the narrow road by a path called repentance. John wrote in **1 John 1:8–9.**

*If we claim*_____

_____.

WHAT ABOUT YOU?

A beautiful example of God's forgiveness is found in Jesus' parable of the prodigal son in Luke 15:11–24. Read the parable.

Verse 13.

Where might your own "far country" be? _____

Is it easier to sin away from home? If so, why? _____

What might prodigals waste other than money? ____ Health ____Self–esteem ____ Talents

____ Opportunities ____ Character ____ Time ____ Other _____

Verse 14. Everyone has needs, but *having* needs is different from being "in need." Have you ever been "in need?" If so, how did you feel?_____

Who, if anyone, met your need?_____

Verse 17. *"He came to his senses."* The prodigal returned home when he was forced to either face himself or cease being human, proving there is no place we can go to escape God. Sooner or later, He catches up with us.

Was there ever a time of self–discovery for you? _____

Did you come face to face with God, and confess, and repent? If so, how did you feel afterward?

_____

The prodigal returned home. Would just "being sorry" have been sufficient?_____

Verse 20. The father, representing God, responded out of love and grace. Was the prodigal still his father's son? _____ The prodigal disrupted fellowship with his father, but the relationship was still intact. Review John 10:28–29.

RESPONSE

Pray Psalm 51 to God, thanking Him for His grace and forgiveness each time you have left the narrow road for the broad road, even for a short time.

Jesus said in **John 6:44**, "_____."

Whenever we feel drawn to Christ and His way of life, we can know the Spirit is drawing us to God either for salvation, for time alone with Him, or to return to Him after going astray.

RUNNING TOWARD THE GOAL

Paul, writing **Philippians 3:12–14**, presented a beautiful picture of the Christian life as one running toward a goal. He wrote, *"Not that I have already obtained all this … but I press on to take hold of that for which Christ Jesus took hold of me.… Forgetting what is behind* _____

_____

_____."

Notice that Paul wrote that he was forgetting the good along with the bad in his past. He wouldn't glory in past achievements as an excuse for relaxing in the future. The Greek word *epekteinomenos* describes the racer straining toward the tape, focused on nothing but the goal. With arms clawing the air, his head forward, and his body bent and angled toward the goal, he runs hard for the finish.[4]

REFLECTING...

I ask myself often: Am I running hard to attain the *"prize for which God has called me heavenward in Christ Jesus"*? When my race is over, will I want to go? Will I have "dying grace"? I long to see Jesus, but I confess I don't want to leave the world today. I prefer to live to a very old age and have Jesus return just before my name is called.

During my childhood my family went annually to the State Fair. After seeing the exhibits and animals, we headed for the midway. My father purchased tickets to last the afternoon. I often tugged on his arm as we waited in line for the anticipated thrills.

"Let me hold my ticket," I would beg.

"I'll give you your ticket when it's time to ride," he would reply.

On occasion, I think of death and pray, "Lord, give me dying grace now." He answers, "You don't need it now. You'll have it when it's time to go. In the meantime, run your race."

Jesus assured us in John 14:1–3: *"Do not let your hearts be troubled. Trust in God; trust also in me. In my Father's house are many rooms; if it were not so, I would have told you. I am going there to prepare a place for you. And if I go and prepare a place for you, I will come back and take you to be with me that you also may be where I am."*

Underline every phrase in that passage that assures and comforts you.

OUR CHEERLEADERS

Paul said *we are surrounded by such a great cloud of witnesses.* (Hebrews 12:1). He pictured the galleries filled with an innumerable throng who, before us, ran the race we now run. Hebrews 11 lists many great biblical runners who are in the grandstands cheering us on to the finish line.

What a group! Take pride in their company. Beginning with Hebrews 11:4, list those whose names follow the words, "*By faith*_____

_____

_____."

Circle those with whose experiences you best identify, remembering that they also identify with you. We cannot see their faces, but we hear their cheers from the pages of Scripture and the accounts of their lives. They cheer us on, anticipating the day when we will join them in heaven.[5]

REFLECTING...

The founders of our faith and the martyrs for the cause of Christ are in the stands cheering. Christian soldiers who died in wars to secure my freedom are there. I hear the voices of my grandparents who died before I was born. Best of all I hear the voices of my parents who gave me life and watched me grow, who nursed me when I was sick, who waited at the side of difficult streams to help me cross, who prayed for me, sacrificed, and were always in my corner.

In heaven ahead of me, they cheer me on: "Run! Run!"

Why are they interested in how I run? Because they have 20–20 spiritual vision. The moment they died and saw Jesus, they had perfect knowledge of what is important and what is not. They know how worthless the trinkets are that would distract me from my race.[6]

WHAT ABOUT YOU?

Name those whose voices you hear cheering you as you run your race of life.

_____

_____

HINDRANCES

The author of Hebrews urges, "*Let us throw off everything that hinders and the sin that so easily entangles....*"

- **The Past.** Consider the past as prologue. Build upon it without boasting about past successes or brooding over outgrown yesterdays.
- **Regrets.** Concentrate not on what might have been, but on what still can be.
- **Sin.** Don't tolerate sin. Confess it, repent, forsake it, and forget.

RUN WITH PERSEVERANCE

Let us run with perseverance the race marked out for us. (Hebrews 12:1)

Since our race is tailor–made, our part is choosing whether to run and how well we will run.

A race has three parts: The start, the middle, and the finish. The start, salvation, is easiest because adrenaline is flowing. The finish is exciting because the crowds cheer us on toward the goal. The middle of the race is hardest, but it's the period when we mature in our faith. To keep us from tiring and losing our focus, the writer of Hebrews urged us to *"fix our eyes on Jesus, the author and perfecter of our faith...."* (v. 2) [7]

ARE WE THERE YET?

Paul wrote, *"Not that I have already obtained all this ... but I press on to take hold of that for which Christ Jesus took hold of me.... Forgetting what is behind and straining toward what is ahead, I press on toward the goal to win the prize for which God has called me heavenward in Christ Jesus"* (Philippians 3:12–14).

As excited children, we measured our growth and recorded our height, with the knowledge that we could never subtract an inch from it. Spiritual growth is also progressive, never decreasing. I pray for your continued growth as I pray for mine, *"until we all reach unity in the faith and in the knowledge of the Son of God and become mature, attaining to the whole measure of the fullness of Christ"* (Ephesians 4:13).

FINALLY...

Maturing is running. It's pressing hard and remaining focused on the goal that the author of *Hebrews* called *"the prize for which God has called me heavenward in Christ Jesus"* (Philippians

3:14). As you run toward your goal, don't be distracted by the world around you or even by other Christians running alongside you. It's your race you're running, not theirs.

Before reaching your goal you may have to endure rugged paths and steep climbs. There will be hurdles to leap and rivers to cross, temptations to conquer and battles to win. So don't run in your own strength, but in the strength of Jesus who said, *"Apart from me you can do nothing"* (John 15:5).

Let Him fill your heart with love, your mind with truth, your soul with peace, and your whole being with fresh vigor. Listen to the cheers of those who have finished their race. Keep your eyes on Jesus, *"the author and perfecter of our faith"* (Romans 12:2). He waits for you at the finish line with your crown of life in His hands. The prize will be worth your struggle, so don't stop, slow down, or fall asleep!

Run, Christian! Run!

LEARNING TO TALK

REFLECTING...

As the youngest of eight children, I was allowed to talk baby talk for years. My family, thinking it cute, often used my mispronounced words when conversing with me. These misnomers became stumbling blocks for me later when I needed to know correct pronunciations and meanings.

After becoming a Christian, I found the language of the Church just as baffling. Unfamiliar words in Scripture, hymns, and praise songs left me clueless as to their meanings. Therefore, I missed opportunities to share Christ with others because I hadn't learned to talk the Christian language. Every discipline has its lingo. Christianity is no exception.

I remember the day I invited my work supervisor to my church. He was in his car at the end of the day.

"No, thanks!" he snorted. "The last time I went to church the congregation sang about a fountain filled with blood drawn from Emmanuel's veins.[1] I told my wife that was the last time I would attend her cannibalistic church!" With that, he spun his car's tires and peeled out of the parking lot. Soon he received a job promotion and moved away. I lost contact with him along with the opportunity to share my faith in Christ with one for whom Christ died.

Frustrated, and feeling God must be disappointed in me, I began collecting definitions of unfamiliar theological terms I heard during worship and Bible study, rewriting them in my own words.

In this chapter I've included some terms I find new Christians need most when learning to talk the language of faith.

WHAT ABOUT YOU?

Jesus wants your help in carrying out His plan to save the world, and He stated as much. Paul said that the Gospel is *the power of God for the salvation of everyone....* (Romans 1:16)

God's intends for you to spread the good news of the Gospel! You must learn the language of Christians in order to convey Christ's message and obey His command in Matthew 28:19–20.

NOW WHAT?

Glance first at the entire list of terms without reading their definitions. Using a pencil, put a check by those you cannot presently define. As you learn their meanings, erase your marks. By memorizing a few definitions each week, you'll soon master them all.

GLOSSARY

Atonement: The act of being brought into "at–one–ment" with God as a result of Christ's sacrificial death on the cross. Our sin demanded the penalty of death, which would have resulted in eternal estrangement from God; but Jesus became our substitute on the Cross so that we can be reconciled to God. *This is love: not that we loved God, but that he loved us and sent his Son as an atoning sacrifice for our sins* (1 John 4:10).

Baptism: The outward expression of an inner experience by which believers identify with Christ and His Church, symbolic of the believer's sharing Christ's death, burial, and resurrection – the washing away of sin. *Therefore go and make disciples of all nations, baptizing them in the name of the Father and of the Son and of the Holy Spirit* (Matthew 28:19).

Belief: The act of accepting by faith that Jesus, the sinless Son of God, paid the penalty for our sins by dying in our place, resulting in our salvation. *They replied, "Believe in the Lord Jesus, and you will be saved..."* (Acts 16:31).

Born again: A condition Jesus described as the new spiritual nature one receives at the moment of salvation. Jesus said, *"You must be born again"* (John 3:7).

Christian: A follower of Christ, literally, a "little Christ;" one who, realizing that he is a sinner and therefore not right with God, trusts Jesus as Savior, unites with Christ by faith, and devotes his life in obedience to God. *The disciples were called Christians first at Antioch* (Acts 11:26).

Confession: An admission of the truth of something. *He who conceals his sins does not prosper, but whoever confesses and renounces them finds mercy* (Proverbs 28:13). *It is with your heart that you believe and are justified, and it is with your mouth that you confess and are saved* (Romans 10:10). *Therefore, holy brothers, who share in the heavenly calling, fix your thoughts on Jesus, the apostle and high priest whom we confess* (Hebrews 3:1).

Conversion: A turning from unbelief to faith, representing a profound inward change in one's character and life that is evidenced by outward change. *Repent, then, and turn to God (be converted), so that your sins may be wiped out...* (Acts 3:19).

Conviction: The realization of the need to break with sin. Conviction begins with unrest over individual guilt that makes one want to stop following the path of sin. Those not convicted of sin in this life will be convicted at the Second Coming of Christ, who will come *to judge everyone, and to convict all the ungodly of all the ungodly acts they have done...* (Jude 15).

Disciple: A learner (student) and follower of Christ. *Therefore go and make disciples of all nations, baptizing them in the name of the Father and of the Son and of the Holy Spirit* (Matthew 28:19). See Matthew 10.

Doubt: Uncertainty; questioning. *Immediately Jesus reached out his hand and caught him. "You of little faith," he said, "why did you doubt?"* (Matthew 14:31).

Eternal life: Life now and forever, resulting from a personal and faith–based relationship with God through Jesus Christ. *The wages of sin is death, but the gift of God is eternal life in Christ Jesus our Lord* (Romans 6:23).

Faith: Belief in action; taking God at His Word with unqualified commitment based on evidence that goes beyond reason but not against it. Faith takes over when understanding has run its course. *Faith is being sure of what we hope for and certain of what we do not see* (Hebrews 11:1).

Glory: God's moral perfection on display; the outshining of God's attributes. *We, who ... reflect the Lord's glory, are being transformed into his likeness with ever–increasing glory, which comes from the Lord, who is the Spirit* (2 Corinthians 3:18). Glory can refer to a position of honor and authority. It can also refer to heaven.

Gospel: The incredible "good news" of God's love shown by sending His Son into the world to redeem the world. *I am not ashamed of the gospel, because it is the power of God for the salvation of everyone who believes* (Romans 1:16).

Grace: Unearned and undeserved favor of God, derived from His undying love. *It is by grace you have been saved, through faith – and this not from yourselves, it is the gift of God – not by works, so that no one can boast* (Ephesians 2:8).

Holiness: The state of the divine nature of God; being without blemish; the fruit of the Spirit's indwelling believers. *Worship the LORD in the splendor of his holiness* (Psalm 29:2).

Holy: Different and separate from that which is not divine. *Therefore, I urge you, brothers, in view of God's mercy, to offer your bodies as living sacrifices, holy and pleasing to God – this is your spiritual act of worship* (Romans 12:1).

Hope: Faith that stretches in its outlook to the future, like an anchor pulling us forward to confidence, assurance, and certainty. *We have this hope as an anchor for the soul, firm and secure...* (Hebrews 6:19).

Intercession: Prayer in the interest of another. *Christ Jesus, who died – more than that, who was raised to life – is at the right hand of God and is also interceding for us* (Romans 8:34).

Justice: The principle of moral rightness; fairness. *Hate evil, love good; maintain justice in the courts* (Amos 5:15).

Justification: More than forgiveness, it includes being cleared of the penalty for sin. If someone harms me, I can forgive him, but I don't have the authority to clear him of the deed. By Christ's death, I am not only forgiven, but I am cleared of my sin. I am justified (just–as–if–I'd never sinned). Paul said, *"Those he called, he also justified; those he justified, he also glorified"* (Romans 8:30).

Kingdom of God: The realm where God reigns supremely as King of kings and Lord of lords; where God's will is perfectly done. Because we live in a sinful world, the kingdom of God will come in its fullness only in heaven. (See Revelation 12:10.) *The kingdom of God is within you* (Luke 17:21).

Knowledge: The insight to know how to handle life situations, gained by learning from Christ what life and God and eternity are all about. *I myself am convinced, my brothers, that you yourselves are full of goodness, complete in knowledge and competent to instruct one another* (Romans 15:14).

Lord: Master, ruler, owner, controller. Jesus asked, *"Why do you call me, 'Lord, Lord,' and do not do what I say?"* (Luke 6:46)

Lost: The state of being separated from God because of unconfessed and unforgiven sin. Jesus said, *"The Son of Man came to seek and to save what was lost"* (Luke 19:10).

Love: The transforming and saving action of God in showing compassion and forgiveness toward sinners. *This is how God showed his love among us: He sent his one and only Son into the world that we might live through him* (1 John 4:9).

Mercy: Compassionate treatment by God because of His kind and forgiving nature toward sinners who deserve justice instead. Jesus said, *"Blessed are the merciful, for they will be shown mercy"* (Matthew 5:7).

New Birth: Entrance into new life in Christ, born from above by the Spirit of God and the Word of God. Jesus declared, *"I tell you the truth, no one can see the kingdom of God unless he is born again"* (John 3:3).

Prayer: Talking to God; listening to God; communing with God. *The prayer of a righteous man is powerful and effective* (James 5:16).

Reconciliation: The bringing together of two estranged parties who should have been together all along. Being estranged from God because of sin, we were brought back into fellowship with God through Jesus' death on the Cross. *All this is from God, who reconciled us to himself through Christ and gave us the ministry of reconciliation: that God was reconciling the world to himself in Christ, not counting men's sins against them* (2 Corinthians 5:18–19).

Redemption: Payment to buy back or to redeem a condemned individual from eternal death by Christ on the Cross. *In him we have redemption through his blood, the forgiveness of sins, in accordance with the riches of God's grace…* (Ephesians 1:7).

Repentance: Unconditional surrender, the turning from one's sin to faith in God, making a 180–degree turn from every thought, word, deed, and habit known to be wrong. Repentance results in a reversal of behavior and change in what one does and the purpose of one's life. *I am happy, not because you were made sorry, but because your sorrow led you to repentance* (2 Corinthians 7:9).

Righteousness: Holiness, justification, integrity; being sinless in the eyes of God; the condition resulting from salvation by the declaration of faith in Christ. *This righteousness from God comes through faith in Jesus Christ to all who believe* (Romans 3:22).

Salvation: The rescue of a person from the penalty and power of sin, and from the presence of sin in the life to come, by Jesus' becoming our substitute on the Cross. *Salvation is found in no one else, for there is no other name under heaven given to men by which we must be saved"* (Acts 4:12).

Sanctification: Progressive growth in holiness and conformity to the character of Christ; the act of being set apart by God for a purpose. Jesus prayed for His followers: *"Sanctify them by the truth; your word is truth. As you sent me into the world, I have sent them into the world. For them I sanctify myself, that they too may be truly sanctified"* (John 17:17–19).

Saved: The state of being rescued from the penalty of sin by accepting Jesus as our substitute on the Cross. The Philippian jailer asked, *"Sirs, what must I do to be saved?" They replied, "Believe in the Lord Jesus, and you will be saved…"* (Acts 16:30–31).

Sin: Living independently from God and missing the mark of God's will by choosing to go one's own way. The sin of unbelief or rebellion against God separates a person from God's presence and blessing, placing the sinner under God's wrath. Paul said, *"All have sinned and fall short of the glory of God"* (Romans 3:23).

Sins: Actions contrary to God's holiness that interrupt a Christian's fellowship with God. *If we confess our sins, he is faithful and just and will forgive us our sins and purify us from all unrighteousness* (1 John 1:9).

Spiritual Birth: The beginning of the spiritual life. The moment of receiving the divine birth and the divine nature through faith in God. Jesus said, *"Flesh gives birth to flesh, but the Spirit gives birth to spirit. You should not be surprised at my saying, 'You must be born again'"* (John 3:6–7).

Trust: A moment–by–moment habit of relying upon God, whatever the circumstances. *Trust in the LORD with all your heart and lean not on your own understanding; in all your ways acknowledge him, and he will make your paths straight* (Proverbs 3:5–6).

Witness: As stewards of the gospel, Christians are to make known what we have seen and heard. Newborn Christians should not delay telling what God has done in their lives. Their salvation experience was sufficient to save them; it will prove sufficient to encourage others to accept Christ. Jesus said, *"You will receive power when the Holy Spirit comes on you; and you will be my witnesses in Jerusalem, and in all Judea and Samaria, and to the ends of the earth"* (Acts 1:8).

END NOTES

LESSON 1

[1] William Barclay, *The Daily Study Bible, The Gospel of Matthew, Vol. 1,* (Philadelphia: The Westminster Press, 1958), pp. 52–53.

[2] Ibid, p. 53.

[3] Wayne Dehoney, *Preaching to Change Lives* (Nashville: Broadman Press, 1974), p. 41.

[4] Croft M. Pentz, *The Complete Book of Zingers* (Wheaton: Tyndale House Publishers, Inc., 1990).

[5] William Barclay, *The Daily Study Bible, The Gospel of John, Vol. I* (Edinburgh: The Saint Andrew Press, 1957), p. 122.

[6] Ibid. pp. 122–123.

[7] Dehoney, op. cit., p. 31.

[8] Bickel, Bruce and Jantz, Stan, *Bruce & Stan's Guide to God,* (Eugene OR: Harvest House Publishers, 1997), p. 211.

[9] Ephesians 4:15.

LESSON 2

[1] David H. C. Read, *Sons of Anak* (New York: Charles Scribner's Sons, 1964), pp. 127–128.

[2] Franklin Graham, *The Name* (Nashville: Thomas Nelson Publishers, 2002), pp. 83–84.

[3] Dennis E. Hensley, *"What's in a Name?" Evangel, Vol. 105, No. 48* (Indianapolis: Free Methodist Communications, December 2, 2001), p. 8.

[4] T. T. Crabtree, *The Zondervan Pastor's Annual for 1968* (Grand Rapids: Zondervan Publishing House, 1968), p.113.

[5] William Barclay, *The Daily Study Bible, The Acts of the Apostles,* (Philadelphia: The Westminster Press, 1955), pp. 93–94.

[6] Hight C. Moore, *From Pentecost to Patmos* (Nashville: Convention Press, 1959), pp. 38–39.

[7] Homer A. Kent, Jr., *Jerusalem to Rome, Studies in Acts* (Grand Rapids: Baker Book House, 1972), p. 99.

[8] Barclay, Op. cit., p. 94.

LESSON 3

[1] Fanny Crosby, 1820–1915, *"Blessed Assurance, Jesus Is Mine."*

[2] Johnson Oatman, Jr., 1856–1922, "Higher Ground."

[3] Psalm 121:4

[4] John 20:28

[5] Alfred Tennyson, as quoted by Georgia Harkness, *Understanding the Christian Faith* (Nashville: Abingdon Press, 1947), p.19.

[6] William Barclay, *The Daily Study Bible: The Letters to the Corinthians* (Edinburgh: The Saint Andrew Press, 1957), p.139.

[7] John Bisagno, *The Word of the Lord* (Nashville: Broadman Press, 1973), p. 90.

[8] Robert J. Dean, *First Corinthians for Today* (Nashville: Broadman Press, 1972), pp. 46–47.

[9] Pearl Buck, quoted by William Walter Warmath, *When He Calls Me* (Nashville: Broadman Press, 1969), p. 66.

[10] Jim Thomas, *Streetwise Spirituality* (Eugene, OR: Harvest House Publishers, 2001), p. 82.

LESSON 4

[1] C. Austin Miles, 1868–1946, *In the Garden,* Public Domain.

[2] William Barclay, *The Daily Study Bible, The Letters to Philippians, Colossians and Thessalonians* (Edinburgh: The Saint Andrew Press, 1960), pp. 78–79.

[3] Jack R. Taylor, *Prayer: Life's Limitless Reach* (Nashville: Broadman Press, 1977), p. 42, quoting Armin R. Gesswein, *Seven Wonders of Prayer* (Grand Rapids: Zondervan, 1957), p. 11.

[4] Alexander MacLaren, quoted by John Allan Lavender, *Why Prayers Are Unanswered* (Valley Forge: The Judson Press, 1967), Frontispiece.

[5] Waylon B. Moore, *Mentoring Disciples in the Local Church Notebook* (Tampa: Missions Unlimited Publishers, 1979), p. 170.

[6] Ibid., p. 171.

[7] Ibid.

[8] Ibid., p. 172

[9] Evelyn Christenson, *A Journey into Prayer* (Colorado Springs: Chariot Victor Publishing, 1995), p. 22.

[10] Anonymous, quoted by Brian L. Harbour, *A New Look at the Book* (Nashville: Broadman Press, 1985), p. 67.

LESSON 5

[1] Jack Kuhatschek, *Taking the Guesswork Out of Applying the Bible* (Downers Grove, IL: InterVarsity Press, 1990), pp. 19–20.

[2] Psalm 119:102.

[3] Henrietta C. Mears, *What the Bible Is All About* (Glendale, CA: Regal Books Division, Gospel Light Publications, 1975), p. 7.

[4] Skip Heitzig, *How to Study the Bible and Enjoy It* (Wheaton: Tyndale House Publishers, Inc., 2002), p. 9.

[5] Billy Beacham, *Back to the Basics Leader's Guide* (Fort Worth: Student Discipleship Ministries, 1988), p. 37, quoting Rick Warren, *"Saddleback Valley Baptist Church"* (Mission Viejo, California), p. 37.

[6] Herschel H. Hobbs, *An Exposition of the Four Gospels, Volume 2, The Gospel of Mark* (Grand Rapids: Baker Book House, 1970, p. 68.

LESSON 6

[1] John Dawson, *Taking Our Cities for God* (Lake Mary, Florida: Creation House, 1989), p. 59.

[2] Joni Eareckson Tada, quoted in Jim Thomas, *Streetwise Spirituality* (Eugene, OR: Harvest House Publishers, 2001), p. 119.

[3] Anne and Ray Ortlund, *You Don't Have to Quit* (Nashville: Thomas Nelson Publishers, 1994), p. 101.

[4] Jack R. Taylor, *The Word of God with Power* (Nashville: Broadman & Holman Publishers, 1993), pp. 96–99.

[5] Ibid., pp. 101–102.

[6] Peter M. Lord, *The 2959 Plan* (Titusville, FL: Agape Ministries, 1982), p. 35. Used by permission.

[7] David C. George, *Layman's Bible Book Commentary, 2 Corinthians, Galatians, Ephesians, Volume 21* (Nashville: Broadman Press, 1979), page 137.

[8] Wiersbe, op. cit., p.168.

[9] Ibid., pp. 168–169.

[10] George Duffield, Jr., 1818–1888, Public Domain

[11] David C. George, op. cit., p. 138.

[12] Evelyn Christenson, *A Journey into Prayer* (Colorado Springs: Chariot Victor Publishing, 1995), pp. 11–12.

LESSON 7

[1] Warren W. Wiersbe, *Be Free,* (Wheaton, IL: Victor Books, 1977), pp. 135–136.

[2] Bill Bright, *Have You Made the Wonderful Discovery of the Spirit–Filled Life?* (Orlando: NewLife Publications, 1995).

[3] Quoted from *Ministers Manual 1981 Edition,* Charles L. Wallis, Editor (San Francisco: Harper & Row, Publishers, 1980), p. 255.

[4] Edward Hastings, Editor, *The Speaker's Bible, The Epistle to the Galatians* (Grand Rapids: Baker Book House, 1963), p. 78.

[5] Ibid.

[6] William Barclay, *The Daily Study Bible, The Letters to the Galatians and Ephesians* (Edinburgh: The Saint Andrew Press, 1959), pp. 56–57.

[7] Warren W. Wiersbe, op.cit., p.136.

[8] Ibid.

LESSON 8

[1] Jack R. Taylor, *The Word of God with Power* (Nashville: Broadman & Holman Publishers, 1993), pp. 113–114.

[2] Ibid., p. 115.

[3] Billy Graham, *The Holy Spirit* (Waco, TX: Word Books Publisher, 1978), p. 139.

LESSON 9

[1] Maxie D. Dunnam, *The Communicator's Commentary, Volume 2, Exodus* (Waco: Word Books, Publisher, 1987), p. 248.

[2] John Bisagno, *Positive Obedience* (Grand Rapids: Zondervan Publishing House, 1979), p. 16.

[3] Ibid., p. 18.

[4] Maxie D. Dunnam, op. cit., p. 260.

[5] Ibid., p. 259.

[6] Dan Betzer, *The Ten Commandments* (Springfield, MO: The General Council of the Assemblies of God and Revivaltime Media Ministries, 1990), p. 18.

[7] Ibid., p. 19.

[8] William Barclay, *The Old Law & the New Law* (Philadelphia: The Westminster Press, 1974), p. 28.

[9] Ibid., p. 30.

[10] Clovis G. Chappell, *Ten Rules for Living* (Nashville: Abingdon Press, 1938), pp.133–134.

[11] Dan Betzer, op. cit., p. 28.

LESSON 10

[1] Warren W. Wiersbe, *Meet Your King* (Wheaton, IL: Victor Books, 1981), p. 185.

[2] William Barclay, *And Jesus Said* (Edinburgh: The Church of Scotland Youth Committee, 1960), p.105.

[3] William Barclay, *The Daily Study Bible, The Gospel of Luke* (Edinburgh: the Saint Andrew Press, 1958), p. 141.

[4] George A. Buttrick, *The Parables of Jesus* (Grand Rapids: Baker Book House, 1977), pp.150–151.

[5] Ibid., p. 151.

[6] William Barclay, *The Daily Study Bible, The Gospel of Matthew* (Philadelphia: The Westminster Press, 1958), p. 359.

LESSON 11

[1] Warren W. Wiersbe, *Meet Your King* (Wheaton: Victor Books, 1981), pp. 213–214.

[2] Myron S. Augsburger, *The Communicator's Commentary: Matthew* (Waco: Word Books, Publisher, 1982), p. 330.

[3] Ron Hutchcraft, *Called to Greatness* (Chicago: Moody Press, 2001), p. 48.

[4] Ibid., p. 49.

[5] William Barclay, *The Daily Study Bible, The Gospel of Matthew, Volume 1* (Philadelphia: The Westminster Press, 1958), p. 363.

[6] Bill Bright, *Have You Heard of the Four Spiritual Laws?* (Orlando: NewLife Publications, 2000), Campus Crusade for Christ, Inc.)

[7] Ron Hutchcraft, op. cit., p. 69.

LESSON 12

[1] Charles R. Swindoll, *Growing Up in God's Family* (Fullerton, CA: Insight for Living), p. 22.

[2] Ibid., pp. 22–23.

[3] Brainerd Duffield, *Alice in Wonderland, a Three–Act Play Adapted from Lewis Carroll's Story* (Boston: Baker's Plays, 1978), p. 25.

[4] William Barclay, *The Daily Study Bible, The Letters to the Philippians, Colossians and Thessalonians* (Edinburgh: The Saint Andrew Press, 1960), p. 82.

[5] Gene Cunningham, *The Basics* (Bigelow, AR: American Inland Mission, Inc., 1990), p. 120.

[6] Ibid.

[7] Ibid. p. 123.

LESSON 13

[1] "There Is a Fountain Filled With Blood" by William Cowper, 1731–1800, Public Domain.